GENDER IDENTITY GUIDE FOR TEENS

How to clear confusion, overcome fear, discover who you truly are and live as your most authentic self today

---

SOPHIA DANIELS

Sophia Daniels

© Copyright 2022 by Sophia Daniels- All rights reserved.

The content contained within this book may not be reproduced, duplicated or transmitted without direct written permission from the author or the publisher.

Under no circumstances will any blame or legal responsibility be held against the publisher, or author, for any damages, reparation, or monetary loss due to the information contained within this book. Either directly or indirectly.

Legal Notice:

This book is copyright protected. This book is only for personal use. You cannot amend, distribute, sell, use, quote or paraphrase any part, or the content within this book, without the consent of the author or publisher.

Disclaimer Notice:

Please note the information contained within this document is for educational and entertainment purposes only. All effort has been executed to present accurate, up to date, and reliable, complete information. No warranties of any kind are declared or implied. Readers acknowledge that the author is not engaging in the rendering of legal, financial, medical or professional advice. The content within this book has been derived from various sources. Please consult a licensed professional before attempting any techniques outlined in this book.

By reading this document, the reader agrees that under no circumstances is the author responsible for any losses, direct or indirect, which are incurred as a result of the use of information contained within this document, including, but not limited to, — errors, omissions, or inaccuracies.

Contents

Introduction	v
1. GENDER IDENTITY	1
How Do You Feel?	10
2. TEENS IN A BINARY WORLD	12
True Story Alert!	13
What About Your Family?	16
What About Your Friends?	17
Fear! It's A Thing!	19
Social Media – A Blessing or Curse?	21
Ways To Help You Start A Discussion	22
Let's Get To Work!	24
Time For You – Grab A Pen	26
Now For The EUREKA Moment!	28
Practical Tips That Can Help	29
You've Come A Long Way	31
Contemplation	33
3. EXERCISES TO DISCOVER AND CELEBRATE WHO YOU REALLY ARE	35
Discover You	39
It Doesn't Have To Be That Way	45
Next... The Practical!	48
Celebrate Your New Thought Process!	51
Self-Celebration!	64
What Self-Celebration is NOT	65
Diary / Journaling	65
Ways To Ground and Be Yourself Authentically	66
Remember	68
Top Tips For Doing These Exercises Yourself!	69
Contemplation	69
4. Q&A AND RESOURCES	71
The Questions	73
Medical Treatments	75
Remember	81

When It All Gets A Bit Much	98
What Do I Want From My Life?	99
Social Media Talk	105
- A Note From Me -	106
This Book Has No Expiry Date	107

Introduction

'Everything is going to be alright.'

How many times has someone said that to you? Once? Twice? Maybe never. More importantly, do you believe it?

Life, for many, can be difficult. It can be challenging to make friends, find your confidence, or discover your voice when you need it the most. Sometimes people struggle with figuring out what they want to do for a living or which course to study at college or university. However, these are relatable to a wide range of people, and there is so much out there to support all of the above and help those who need to make choices that help develop them as a person.

What about gender identity?

It's safe to say; that we are living in a world that is slowly yet surely becoming more open to the discussion surrounding gender identity with each passing day. You'll frequently notice that more places of work and school are accepting of the correct use of pronouns and respect the choices of those who wish to be addressed a certain way. But does that make it easier for *you* to understand your own mind and body?

I think you'll agree, it isn't that easy, and it may not be for you.

You see, not everybody is blessed with a loving and supportive family. We aren't all cut from the crust of understanding or even awareness of just how much the topic of gender identity is filtering through into society, in the urge to be more open and transparent about it. That, in turn, can make it extremely difficult for you to figure out who you are, but there is one thing you should remember.

It's alright to not have all the answers at the moment.

I can't stress that enough, and if you need to come back and read that phrase as you work through the book, then do so.

If you want a little reassurance, I will extend this phrase with the following. Any, yes, *any,* person of teenage years goes through confusing times. Bodies change, hormones develop, moods come and go, and confusing thoughts enter your mind about the next stage of your life or who you become attracted to. You'll have the pressure of school and wanting to do well, the fear of letting your family down, and I'll even trump those with the grand old concept of peer pressure. 'What are my friends doing?' 'Should I be doing what they are, just because they are?'

Believe me when I say I do not speak *at* you. I speak from those awkward and sometimes painful experiences that all teenagers have. The huge difference now is that not all teenagers find the topic of gender identity as confusing, and that is where I feel this book and the exercises I will present to you to be something of a treasure for you.

Introduction

Before I talk about what this book entails, I want you to know that this book is *not* a substitute for therapy. Once you reach the end and read that last word, I want your take-home message to be a deep breath in and a deep breath out, and then I wish for your inner voice to change from, 'What on earth are these strange thoughts or feelings?' to, 'Everything is going to be alright.'

In this book, you may not think it possible, but I have mixed the most thoughtful advice with relatable examples for you, particularly if you feel alone or misunderstood in your process or experience.

In each chapter, I will offer you some tools to help your confusion or anxiety, because, let's all be honest here, anxious feelings lead to anxious thoughts, and anxious thoughts lead to overthinking. It's like a hamster wheel you don't want to be on, which can be destructive.

There is nothing wrong with wanting to be yourself, but it can seem frustrating if you don't know who that is. The 'identity' in gender identity is you. Therefore it can be easy to feel the pressure of not knowing who that person is.

These bodies we live in are our homes. We take them wherever we go. School, the cinema, our friend's house, or the supermarket. What is the one thing we all naturally want? We want to feel safe in our homes, which can cause untold amounts of uncertainty if we don't.

This is why I hope you find these topics relevant and that they and any guidance to detract from the book will offer you some clarity. You'll read about gender identity with up-to-date information and definitions. You'll learn how to alleviate some of the pressure you feel with simple, day-to-day exercises that will help you manage your feelings. As we

Introduction

go along, you'll be offered the chance to do some real pen-and-paper exercises designed to help you feel more in control and provoke thoughts of reassurance rather than fear.

As the book enters the final chapter, it will be a good opportunity to go through a Q&A section where I answer common questions related to gender identity.

Think of this book as a bit of a toolbox. As you open it, you can frequent yourself with whichever tool you need in order to help you at that moment in time.

As the topic of gender identity becomes more publicly circulated, I wanted to offer you some great resources for both your parents and you. As well as support groups, these will also include social media accounts, so please, use them in ways that help you, because that is precisely what they are designed for. If you do not have access to social media, you will still find the other resources very valuable.

I hope you enjoy the book because you are *not* alone. It is a safe area for you to explore what gender identity means to you. Remember:

It's alright to not have all the answers at the moment.

ONE

Gender Identity

Other than using our name, we identify ourselves using pronouns. She/they, he/him, they/him are all various ways to consider how to identify, which can be very confusing when deciding where you fit. Having such a choice on what matches your identity isn't meant to intimidate or scare you in any way; they are there to offer you the freedom to be the person you want to be, the person you feel you are.

Knowing the answer to that question doesn't happen overnight. Still, I have created an initial list of various gender identities that will help you get to grips with definitions that can help and support you take a few steps closer to exploring your own gender identity.

Before you go through the terminology, I want you to pause for a moment. We live in a world now where we can watch an entire TV series in a day, and whilst it's great to give ourselves so much information, our minds need a bit of time to catch up and really absorb the present moment.

So, not for me, but for you, I'd like you to close your eyes, take a deep breath in for five seconds, and then breathe out for seven. I'd like you to repeat this five times, and as you do so, on each exhale, release any pressure you currently feel and any expectations that may be upon you.

How did that feel? It won't be the last time I ask you to pause because it is a beautiful way to regroup and gather your thoughts.

One thing that would be good to note is that language changes. Some of these terms now are different from those used in the past to describe similar identities. Still, it is important to keep as up-to-date as possible with terminology so that going forward, you can recognise and respect your identity and those of others as the individuals they are.

So now, let's make a start on the terminology you may have heard or may hear going forward.

Sex

Sex refers to a person's biological status. This is typically assigned at birth and usually on the basis of external anatomy. You're going to be familiar with 'male' and 'female,' but there is also *intersex,* which we will look at further down the list. You may notice that some people use *sex* and *gender* somewhat interchangeably because, for many, their sex and gender are the same. However, this isn't the case for many people, so it is important to be able to differentiate between the two.

Gender

With a social construction relating to behaviours and attributes based on labels of either masculinity or femininity, gender is often categorised as either male, female or non-binary. There are variations in how people experience gender, which is based on how you see yourself, and how you express and behave. Remember, this can change, and your pronouns over the years may change too.

Gender Identity

Imagine a line on a piece of paper, with 'man' written on one end and 'woman' written on the other. This line, or spectrum, has room for anything in between, and where you may see yourself can be placed at any point on there.

Gender identity can be a deeply held and essential sense of self and is usually self-identified within each individual. Many don't question theirs and continue their journey onward, but for so many people now, they are questioning if who they feel they are matches with what they see in the mirror.

Now ever increasingly common, gender identity is being understood as something that is not binary, but instead on this spectrum, and growing numbers of people are finding comfort in the notion that they get to decide where they sit on that line. This can initially seem scary, but it is a very empowering place to be.

Gender Expression

How you outwardly present your gender, whether that be how you dress, how you choose to talk, your perceived characteristics or your general behaviour, is how you create your gender expression. For so long now, society has deemed all of these as masculine, feminine, or androgynous to name a few, but we are quickly coming to realise that it just isn't that simple. It hasn't been that simple for a while now and is constantly changing, and especially varies by culture.

Other ways to express your gender are with your chosen name and pronoun, not to mention other physical attributes such as hair and make-up.

Expression is a healthy way for you to be the person you feel comfortable being.

Cisgender (pronounced -sis-gender)

Cisgender is a term used when a person's gender identity matches that of their sex assigned at birth. An easy way to see it is, if you were born female, you remain that way, and if you were born male, you also remain that way.

Cisgendered people's identities match their birth gender, bodies and identity. This does not mean they cannot be a part of the LGBTQIA+ community; it simply means their identity matches their sex and gender.

Transgender

To be a transgender person is to be descriptive of a person whose gender identity, or how their internal sense of being either female, male, or something else, doesn't match the sex they were assigned when they were born. So, for example, a transgender woman would have been labelled as male at birth, and a transgender man would be somebody who was assigned to be female at birth.

Some people don't identify exclusively with one gender and may express both male and female elements within their identity. These transgender people are often described as *non-binary*, which I will discuss in more detail below. Another term for people who fall into this category is *genderqueer*.

Pause
Take a moment.

Non-binary

With many people being raised to believe that gender and sex are the same thing, more than two options are available to us. This is because neither gender nor sex is inherently *binary* – as the belief that people must be boxed into the category of either male or female is becoming more outdated.

Non-binary people usually do not have a fixed gender and are considered *gender fluid*. They experience a variety of masculine, feminine or androgynous identities and do not label their gender as one or the other. There is freedom in identifying as non-binary, and this in no way shapes or confirms your preference when it comes to sexuality. But, again, as with all identities, you can be within or out of the LGBTQIA+ community.

Androgynous (And-rod-gin-us)

Androgyny refers to somebody whose gender expression includes masculine and feminine characteristics. Being androgynous can vary significantly from person to person, as the idea of what a person considers to be masculine or feminine can drastically change in each individual.

You cannot define those who identify as androgynous as either 'looking like a boy' or 'looking like a girl.' It isn't that straightforward, and it is mostly about pure self-expression.

You can be androgynous and be heterosexual, gay, or any other orientation, as it has nothing to do with your sexual preferences and is instead based on gender expression.

Agender

Agender is defined as not having a gender. Therefore, some who identify as being agender may describe it as having a *lack of gender.*

It could be that some simply do not care about gender and don't see it as something that should be at the front of their minds, and that to be labelled as one thing is not what they define as their own gender identity.

Agender people can be of any sexuality and can have any preference to pronouns, although they don't really like to use gendered language.

Gender Transition

Transitioning is a process. When a person transitions, they change the way they look so that the gender you feel on the inside matches the gender you look on the outside.

To transition can mean several things. It can involve medical treatment and hormones, changing your name or pronouns, or your appearance and how you dress. On another level, it can include coming out to your friends and family, which is a huge step and one that you may feel intimidated by if you know this will be you one day.

The process of transitioning can be long and ongoing, or it can happen over a shorter period of time. Not all transgender people transition, and if they do, they may not transition in the same way. You can *socially* transition or *medically* transition. People will have their own views on what transition is, and rather beautifully, there is not one thing a person needs to do to match their identity with their expression, but that is down to the individual.

If you ever find yourself wanting to transition in any way, your process, like all those who go through similar, should be respected, no matter what.

> *Handwritten note:* See also: gender euphoria (happiness) more important + more reliable than dysphoria!

Gender Dysphoria

If a person whose gender identity differs from the sex assigned at birth, or sex-related physical characteristics, a feeling of distress or discomfort can arise, which is called *gender dysphoria.*

Both gender-diverse and transgender people can experience gender dysphoria in their lives, whilst others can live quite at ease.

As this is more of a side effect of realising your gender identity, there are things you'd usually look out for, such as a strong desire to have the genitals of another gender or a strong desire to be treated as another gender.

Gender dysphoria can leave a person feeling significantly distressed, in particular during social occasions, at school or work, or in other areas of their lives. It can come and go and become stronger during fluctuating hormonal changes as your body and mind continue to grow the way biology intended it to, which may not be in line with how you identify.

As gender dysphoria can affect so many aspects of your life, it is essential to reach out if you feel you need to talk to somebody. If you don't feel you can talk to family or friends, support systems are in place, and you can find those numbers at the end of the book.

The stress surrounding these strange feelings can seem overwhelming, but that's because those who go through it are discovering themselves, and sometimes that can take a while to figure out. That doesn't mean there's anything wrong with you; in fact, it's great to gain knowledge about who you are and how you want to identify because it means you value your identity.

Sexual Orientation

You are at the age where you will start to become attracted to people around you, either physically or emotionally or both. It is perfectly natural for you to develop and express your sexuality in healthy ways, regardless of the gender you are attracted to.

Older teenagers may begin relationships or start dating, while younger teens may show signs of curiosity about their sexuality and notice those changes within their bodies.

There are lots of different types of sexuality., and these differ from gender identity. How you identify has nothing to do with your sexual orientation, there are *no right or wrongs.*

Some of the terms young people or children might use to describe their sexual orientation are:

- **Lesbian or gay** – this is when girls are attracted to other girls.

- **Homosexual or gay** – when boys are attracted to other boys.
- **Heterosexual or straight** – When either girls or boys are attracted to a person of the opposite sex.
- **Bisexual** – When a person is attracted to people of either sex.
- **Asexual** – When a person doesn't feel a sexual attraction to anyone.
- **Questioning** – When a person feels unsure about their sexual orientation.

You aren't different for relating to any of those differing terms, even though you may feel it. Society has a great way of putting us all into little boxes and making us feel we should be one thing, but that's far from the reality of modern-day life, and realising that is a huge step towards taking the stress away from your own feelings.

Intersex

A fairly general term used to describe a variety of conditions is *intersex*. This term is frequently used for a variety of conditions whereby a person is born with a reproductive or sexual anatomy that neither fits the description of male or female.

For example, a person may be born appearing to be female on the outside but may have mostly male-typical anatomy on the inside. Another example would be that a person may be born with an anatomy that appears to be between male and female or has noticeably small or large genitals. Sometimes, a person can be born with mosaic genitals, so some cells may have XX chromosomes, and some have XY chromosomes.

Intersex anatomy doesn't always show up at birth, and sometimes these changes don't show up until puberty, which along with the usual teenage roller-coaster of changes, can be a lot to deal with. Some people, however, never know they have intersex anatomy and carry on leading a life oblivious.

Nature doesn't really decide where 'female' ends and 'intersex begins or where 'intersex' begins, and 'female' ends. How you are born is not in your control or anybody else's. Still, as you grow up and get older and decide for yourself how you want to be represented or what help you may reach out for, it is entirely in your control, and there are so many resources that can help you further if you need it, just at the end of the book.

How Do You Feel?

There is a lot of language surrounding gender identity, isn't there? I wonder how many you recognised as you were working your way through the list and how many were new. I also wonder how many you read and thought, 'Oh, I thought it meant *this* instead.'

Check-in with yourself for a moment and have a think about everything you've just read, and if need be, go through it all again.

What do you think when you see the terminology? Do you see yourself relating to any of it?

One thing that is good to remember at this point is that there are many definitions for a reason. There has never been more of a need not only to express yourself fully and the way you internally feel the need to, but there is a huge need to be able to put a name to it.

You might be feeling a mixture of emotions after reading a fair bit of information on how you can personally identify, and that's OK. Whether you are on the cusp of transitioning or simply questioning gender identity as a whole, you may feel as though you aren't being understood. The key to self-discovery is a unique blend of time and knowledge.

You're in no rush to decide how you want to identify, despite the pressures you may feel. Although you may not be blessed with a family who is easy to communicate with or keen to understand what you're going through or even the questions you may have, you aren't alone.

Feeling a certain way about your gender identity may leave you feeling all kinds of things. Anxious, a little down or feeling depressed, or as if nobody understands you.

In the next chapter, I'm going to start providing you with some exercises to do and talk more about how to alleviate the pressures you may be feeling as you go through your teenage years.

TWO

Teens in a Binary World

My intention in writing this book was never to assume that every child comes from a happy, loving home. Too many books these days focus on, 'Wow, so you came out/decided to identify as XYZ and your parents and friends were so happy and supportive of you, really the transition was beautiful, and angels were singing!'... Doesn't that sound lovely? I mean, if I could wish that for everybody, then I think the world would be filled with very happy people who feel validated and accepted, but also a more peaceful world, filled with less hate and more respect.

Unfortunately for many, maybe even you, your home may not be warm. You may not have derived from a place of nurture or understanding, or perhaps your religion omits the concept of gender identity as nothing more than, 'you are who you were born as, no exceptions.'

I wonder how that has made you feel in your journey. Has it made you less likely to admit that you are curious about your own gender identity, or has it made you fearful of even asking questions or starting an honest conversation with your loved ones?

More confusingly, plenty of people come from very secure homes, willed with praise and stability, but their families still do not accept the changing of a person's identity. Or struggle to come to terms with their children deciding they want to transition or express themselves differently from how they've always seen and known them.

True Story Alert!

My best friend at school never dated. He was so much fun to be around; we went out places, sat in the park with our burgers and chips, and in our later teenage years when the law permitted, we went to the pub at the weekend. Our mutual friends often asked us why we didn't go out together, but we laughed it off. In fact, I had a huge crush on another boy, and my friend, let's call him Tom, was very supportive and encouraging of that, so I knew there were no secret romantic feelings between us.

Before we reached those pivotal years of legality, my sixteen-year-old self was sat in my A – Level IT class with him, who was seventeen. He was fairly quiet that day, and I had asked him if everything was alright, to which he replied, 'yes.' A few moments later, Tom pushed his chair back and looked directly at me. 'I need to talk to you,' he said.

With a confused look, I got up and followed him out of class, and as we stood in the school hallway, his jaw clenched.

'I'm gay,' he said. His eyes were wide, and he was so still, you'd think he was a shop mannequin. I looked back at him and saw the panic as he anticipated my response.

'I know,' I replied, with a simple shrug of my shoulders. The thing was, I never consciously thought that Tom was gay. I never sat there thinking, 'my friend is gay,' but there was *something* I had held subconsciously that just gave me the feeling he was, so when he came out to me, I wasn't at all surprised.

'How do you know?' he said. 'I haven't told anyone.'

'Tom, I've known you for years. I know. How does it feel to say it out loud?'

I remember Tom looking at me and inhaling deeply. 'Good,' he said. 'Now I just have to find a way to tell my parents.'

Tom came from a very happy home, with two loving parents and a sweet little brother. His parents were always so polite to me and any other friend who came to their house. The problem only started when Tom decided to tell his parents that he was gay. His mum, tiny in frame, was very quiet, and his dad gave him the silent treatment and disowned him. This caused a lot of friction between the married couple, as Tom's mum wanted, in some way, to support Tom, but wasn't fully given permission to.

There was no strong religion in the household. The reaction of Tom's dad was based purely on his bigoted view that men should marry women, and anything else was simply unacceptable.

Tom was naturally very sad and, for a long time, incorrectly blamed it on his identity ripping apart his relationship with his dad. On reflection, Tom realised it wasn't his identity at all that was the problem; it was the conditional view that a child must be who the parent wants them to be that ripped the relationship apart.

Tom was lucky enough to have a great support system with his maternal grandparents, mum, brother and friends. Still, the breakdown of his relationship with his father was enough to make him realise that coming out can be incredibly difficult and that you never really know how someone you know very well will respond.

My memory of Tom coming out to me is that it was an honour to be considered open, friendly, trusting and accepting enough to be the first person he came to, to tell. From then on, we began talking more openly about it, with him telling me about his crushes and exploring the gay scene in a city nearby.

We had so much fun and always joked when we went out that nobody would want to date us because we were always together and probably looked like a couple! But eventually, we made friends with other gay people, and Tom was able to spend time with people who understood his journey from a relatable point of view.

Tom, in my eyes, was a wonderful friend. Unfortunately, life had us drift apart, but I know after all these years, he is in a happy and long-term relationship with a man, and they are living their best lives. That doesn't, though, detract from the fear and loneliness he felt when he realised he liked boys as a teenager, and it doesn't detract from the difficulties he initially faced with his own family, who have since become more accepting (well, they had no choice!)

So...

What do *you* think about Tom's experience? Has it made you feel angry for him at the time? I know I was. You yourself may not feel the need to come out as gay at all, and some of you might. Gender identity is linked with the LBGTQIA+ community, but is not synonymous with it. You can identify as so many types of person, but it doesn't automatically mean your sexual preferences have changed.

There is, however, a link here in the informing of your loved ones that you wish to be known as (enter your identity here). At this moment in time, you could just be curious about gender identity as a whole, and that's great too. Perhaps you are the 'Me' from 22 years ago who has a friend that needs a little support, or maybe you are even the parent who is looking for some guidance on what it all means.

There is no such thing as 'one size fits all' here. Everyone is welcome, and nobody is judged.

What About Your Family?

When it comes to thinking about your own family, what are your initial thoughts? Do you have particularly narrow-minded parents or siblings? Do you have a grandparent who cannot seem to pull himself or herself to current times and see people as people, not one gender or one sexuality?

I don't even wish to sit here and assume that all of you *have* a family because I know perfectly well this may not be the case. Maybe you're in the care system and are waiting for a foster or adoption process, which means you've met a lot of adults recently and have nobody that you can get to know long enough to be able to talk to them about any questions you may have circulating in your mind.

As if that wasn't enough to contend with, right? Now you have these confusions bombarding you each and every day, and you've no clue which way to turn. Feeling lost and unable to think about who you can talk to probably isn't new for you, as life itself can turn us upside down sometimes, but when you've had no real stability growing up, and a lack of security or real love, time and affection, it can seem all too easy to reject yourself, as if your thoughts don't matter.

They do.

You matter.

You all matter.

My words alone aren't going to suddenly give you that magical 'light bulb' moment, where it all makes sense, and you feel better in the blink of an eye. But what if you considered everything written to be a voice on *your side*. It is that simple. I have no motive other than to encourage you not to feel alone and that right here, right now, is your safe place, where you can be alone with your thoughts and, more so, *trust* them.

What About Your Friends?

To some people, including friends, it may not be simple for them to understand changes that you may one day or have already started to go through. Their only knowledge of gender identity, or any of the terms you've read in the initial glossary, could be a lot less than you to start with.

I would love to think you have a great group of friends or even one or two you consider to be best friends that you can turn to for advice or just to be there for you. I know, though, that it simply isn't the case for many, no matter how old you are.

Whether you are a friend or want to point your friends in this direction, I've thought of a few things that can initially help you/them to be there and show up for those thinking about their gender identity. As I aim to be inclusive and respectful of all situations, if you are personally struggling with friendships, I want you to apply these tips to *yourself*. Yes, you read correctly. Self-love starts today, and I know you have it in you to love yourself.

Research

Seeking out a wide range of knowledge will never not help you. A great place to start is at the end of this book. Try to avoid communities that do not offer factual advice or full support. There are many organisations that can help you in any phase of life, and even your school or college will have something in place for those experiencing gender identity curiosities.

Show Respect

Respect goes a long way. As a friend or loved one, you may feel afraid of making a mistake by offending someone if you use the incorrect pronouns or are unsure which names to use. However, continuously doing so can show that a person is very unsupportive.

Also – a good plan is to avoid the word 'preference.' Preference actually implies a choice, and it isn't really appropriate to use the word when describing someone's identity.

Equally, respect *yourself*, especially if you are reading this for yourself. Don't brush off those gut feelings and ignore what your core identity is trying to communicate with you. Learn that you *can* be who you feel you are. That involves respecting yourself as a person.

Be An Ally

No matter who you are, it is so important to speak up and be open about your support of gender identity and its diverse meaning. Make yourself aware of both issues and services that serve the people who identify differently from you or how you wish to identify, and wherever you are, advocate for policies that serve equal rights for those who don't conform to gender stereotypes, even if that person is you.

If you are at school and you hear somebody saying something offensive, learn just that; that it *is offensive.* Establishments encourage the reporting of behaviour like this. In addition, many laws now prevent people from getting away with hateful behaviour, as it has been deemed a hate crime.

Get Support

Incorporating new information into your understanding of the world may be new to you as you learn about gender identity. Support groups are available to those who have questions or need guidance, and schools or colleges will have a counsellor or mentor, who is there, especially for you, and people in your boat.

Fear! It's A Thing!

How *do* you suppose fear from others towards gender identity can present itself? Tom's dad may have reacted the way he did due to not being taught as a child or teenager growing up what it means to be gay. Remember how just a few generations ago, being gay wasn't as accepted as it is now, despite the hurdles *still* faced today. Therefore, Tom's dad may simply be living his life under his morals and beliefs, with no malice intended for anybody who chooses to live outside his moral compass.

More interestingly, as I've got older (not that old!), I have thought more and more about what it means to have a child or a loved one who decides to identify as someone different to whom they were born as. This could be anything, by the way. Straight, gay, androgynous, non-binary, transgender, etc. My point here is anybody who identifies differently. My thoughts have changed somewhat, but mostly I have felt compassion for people who struggle to hear their loved one is changing. (I use changing from their perspective, not yours. After all, you aren't changing, just simply being more aware of the real 'you.')

My compassion extends to their potential concerns for you. But, sadly, yes, there are people out there who refuse to accept the concept of gender identity and see the world in black and white, without all its glorious colours (hello, pride flag!).

What if, though, they feared for the safety of their loved one? As afraid as you could be of not being accepted by them, they may carry the same fear and extend it into society. What if you hit stumbling blocks? What if you are met with prejudices as you apply for jobs, socialise, or are in a place where you fight for your own equal rights?

Having a loved one react in a way that surprises you (unless it's plain mean) could come from a place of fear. For you, and genuine concern as a loving parent. But, remember that their fear comes from an unknown place, and they may need a little support or guidance on how to show up and be the best they can be.

Social Media - A Blessing or Curse?

I'm not going to talk about the 'old days,' even though they seemed like yesterday to me. I will say that I did not have my first mobile phone until I was sixteen. Hard to believe, isn't it? When I *did* get that phone, all it had was the option to call, send a text (the original way), or play Snake, the one game it had on its memory. I won't knock it, though; it was highly addictive. I digress!

Mobile phones were so we could send the odd text or call our friends or parents and let them know where we were. I have seen the technological advances in phones and what they offer, and I am only too aware that this also means what *content* is on those phones. I used to go home, maybe load my emails, check my MSN to see if any friends were online to chat to briefly, then log off, as my parents may need to use the phone and the modem needed to dial up for the internet interrupted that line (do you believe what you are reading?)

Now though, I have to hand it to you all; you have a blimmin' lot of passwords to remember. TikTok, Instagram, Facebook, Snapchat, Twitter; you name it. I'd love to say I can keep up, and I do have a few social media accounts, but they are used mainly for work and news. Now there are influencers who make *millions* simply by uploading entertaining content, which blows my mind.

You'll have various friends and family or acquaintances on your different social media platforms, and you'll likely follow a lot of people who influence you in some way. Perhaps food pages, a particular sport you like, music or film stars, or maybe you follow certain hashtags to see what is trending and keep up to date with the latest crazes.

With the freedom of being able to find like-minded people online to follow, as there are some really responsible pages that exist for people who have gender identity questions, you can often feel a sense of relief when you extend your curiosity online in the right places. One beautiful thing about the internet is that it brings people together, no matter how many miles between. Everything is so instant, and that can be both, you guessed it, a blessing or a curse.

No matter how old you are, it is essential to be responsible online and recognise when something isn't right. It takes much strength to shake off unwanted comments or opinions, and you will likely encounter those in general. But, as you explore your own feelings and thoughts, you may be inclined to reach out and connect with other curious people, or perhaps those who are further along in their journey of self-discovery, for inspiration, and that's OK.

Just remember to look after yourself online and always be authentic. Reading others' experiences and relating them to yourself is an incredibly empowering thing to do, and I wanted to offer you some great social media accounts to check out, which I have done at the end of the book.

Ways To Help You Start A Discussion

Perhaps you've known for a while that you need to have a discussion with your parents or carers about your gender identity, and you've struggled to think of how to do this, considering it usually isn't something that you discuss over breakfast. However, even the closest families, with parents who think they know their child very well, can be surprised when they learn their son or daughter has gender questions or wishes to transition.

This doesn't mean people won't adjust, and most parents, given a bit of time to think about what they are hearing, will be proud of their child for being able to come to them and speak honestly.

If you are fortunate enough to be able to approach your parents, carers, or a trusted adult on the topic of gender identity, here are some great tips to think about when it comes to that first discussion.

- Decide if you'd rather have both parents present, if you live with both, or if you have a preference with one in particular. If you find it easier to approach one, then that's fine if it works for you. Just ensure the doors to the other are open if the chosen parent needs to talk to them.
- If you do have the chat with one parent, discuss a plan to tell the other, together if necessary, so that there are no secrets.
- If you make any decisions that mean informing your parents, and they are over the moon for you, expect them to ask you if you plan on telling extended family members or friends and how that would make you feel. You have to go at your own pace.
- If you decide on telling your best friend, make sure they can be trusted. Your news shouldn't be shared until you are ready.
- Having a talk about gender identity is a huge thing, and it will only initially happen once. Make sure you are ready, safe and sure that you are prepared for whatever comes next.

Let's Get To Work!

One of the main reasons for my writing this book is to not only provide you with written support and information that may aid any curiosity surrounding gender identity but to equip you with the tools to be able to pinpoint situations that may have affected you and allow you the time be able to be open with yourself, and really think about why it might be this way.

This sort of thought processing can really begin to help shift your attention from the 'it must be me' to 'it isn't me at all,' because essentially, whatever outside negative influence you may be receiving, is not down to an incorrect way that you're living your life.

Have A Think

Can you think of a time, place or situation that left you feeling slightly triggered? I'll give you an example.

Rose is fifteen, and for a year or so, she has begun to explore the possibility that she may wish to change her pronouns to 'they' because she doesn't feel one gender, in particular, is representative of her as a person. She has a group of friends who seemingly have no gender identity issues, and when she mentions a pop star who has recently announced that they would like to be addressed as 'they', her friends laughed and said it was silly.

What do you think Rose would be feeling about that? She would likely be embarrassed, perhaps anxious about telling her friends how her gender expression is changing and that she would really like their support and understanding.

Rose may feel triggered every time a friend mentions this pop star or the fact that people are changing their pronouns, and it might make her feel a fear of not being able to fully be the person she wishes to transition to.

Fear often leads to panic. And for a long time, Rose may begin to experience very low moods or depressive moods. Some people, in their confusion, feel the pain and wish for it to be released, and so they hurt themselves.

So what could Rose do to help herself?

More importantly, what could *you* do if you felt the world wasn't understanding of you? What does panic or anxiety feel like? What does depression feel like?

The Weight of The World

Carrying these immensely difficult and sometimes strange feelings can feel like you are carrying the weight of the world on your shoulders, so if you ever feel particularly anxious or depressed, you need to know that you are not alone. Of course, these feelings can come from feeling excluded or insecure about yourself, but there are so many things to help you.

Depression isn't just about feeling sad. With depression, sadness, or low moods, they do not tend to just go away. You might feel irritable or not interested in the things you used to enjoy. You may feel tired for much of the time but still have trouble sleeping, leading to a lack of concentration. You could find yourself more indecisive, with less interaction with family and friends.

Anxiety can feel like you're on a hamster wheel and you can't get off. Unexplained butterflies or knots in your tummy can make you feel as though something bad will happen, and that only feeds the cycle of worry that you may feel a lot of the time. You also may notice mood changes or back out of social events. Your sleep can also be affected, and you may find it hard to concentrate as your mind overthinks.

What, if anything, could make you feel those things to the point where they start to really affect your life?

- The feeling like you don't belong.
- That the world is a horrible place, and your current confusion is making it worse.
- You feel alone and unsupported.
- You have been targeted or teased due to your identity, thoughts, curiosity and/or opinions on gender identity.

Time For You - Grab A Pen

Now you are sitting comfortably, hopefully, with a pen and paper, or if you have your notes open on your phone, I would like you to make a list of the words that come into your mind when you think about your own gender identity. Of course, these words will differ significantly for all of you, and maybe your own list will have a diverse blend of words, but at this stage, it's about getting all those feelings from your mind to paper (or screen).

What words have you come up with? I made a list of what came to my own mind about me, and I wanted to share mine with you.

- Scary
- Fun
- Uncertain

- Confusing
- Lonely
- Boring
- Plain

At one point or another, I have felt all these things about my own identity. Who I am, how I dress, how I speak, how I present myself, and who I am attracted to. The list goes on. I think it's incorrect to assume we as people, in our 80 or so years of life, will never evolve, change or be curious about who we are, even in some way.

Now, I would like you to think about five sentences that best describe your family/home/friend life. There are no right or wrong ways to do this, and I will write down my examples for you to prove it.

- My partner doesn't really understand me much of the time.
- I have a few close friends who I can talk to, but I don't like to bother them.
- I love my job, but I don't work as part of a team, so I miss out on socialising.
- I am raising my son to be thoughtful of himself and care for his mind and body.
- My father is not kind, so I don't have a relationship with him now I am an adult.

A good list of positives and negatives, I think you'll agree. But here is an excellent example of life not being perfect, and rarely is it so for anyone. When you look at your list, can you relate any of your circumstances to how your gender identity makes you feel? I think about my gender expression and how I don't get many opportunities to go out and dress up for an occasion because I spend a lot of time at home, working on my own, so when I *do* go out, I feel pretty self-conscious, and that what I am wearing or how I look is going to be criticised.

Imagine how it must feel to be transitioning from the person you were to the person you actually *are.* I would probably use most of the words from my first list, especially if it meant I had to then inform my family and friends.

Why do you think it is this way? Can you think of any reasons as to why people may make you feel uncomfortable? I've thought of a few that may crop up in your list, but if they don't, that doesn't invalidate what your list contains.

- Your body is changing through your teenage years.
- Your voice might be changing.
- You may develop spots or notice you sweat more.
- If you have an internal female reproduction system, you may begin to have periods.
- They may have certain opinions about your gender identity, pronouns, or sexuality.
- You may come from a very religious environment, where aspects of gender identity are deemed forbidden.
- You may have unsupportive parents.
- You may be in foster care and have no real person to trust or talk to.
- You may live in an abusive household.

Now For The EUREKA Moment!

Looking at my list alone, it's easy to see that people your age can struggle. But, and it's a big but, If you look at it again, I challenge you to find any of the reasons on that list as to why it is *your* fault. Have a good look back. Your family situation? No. A parent potentially being abusive? No. Your body changing? No.

You see, all these things are out of your control, and trying to put yourself down as the reason why they happen, would be seriously missing the mark.

You're you. You're changing and dealing with everything else that any other person goes through in your life.

When fear leads to panic, we have just as little control.

Remember that breathing exercise we discussed earlier on?

Breathe in slowly for five seconds and out for seven. Repeat five times.

What can you do to alleviate some pressure from your day-to-day life? How can you begin to ease the tension or worry you're feeling?

Practical Tips That Can Help

Firstly, you're going to very likely be enrolled in a school. Every school will have an equal rights policy that it must uphold. It doesn't matter what you think about it or how uncertain you feel about the concept, but your school *will* have something in place and a person to speak with about any concerns you have or feelings you want to explore. This is a practical tip that can help support you in a safe place. And nobody but you and the school has to know.

Each bad thought leads to another. We will look at this in more depth as the book continues, but for now, it's good to make sure you know that one small thought can lead to a catastrophic set of thoughts that play out a worst-case scenario. Believe me when I say that I am only too aware of how damaging these thoughts can be and how difficult it is to 'unbelieve' them.

Small ways to rethink negative thoughts can be turning them on their own head. 'I feel so alone' can be replaced with really practical steps to prove yourself wrong, and that could be your aim. If your thought is that you feel alone and that nobody, truly nobody, is there for you, then make sure you have at least two numbers in your phone or written down on a piece of paper that you can call. You may think, 'well, what friends do I have?' - they don't need to be. The Samaritans or Childline are two numbers that so, so many people use. You may well worry when you hear those words, but honestly, at the end of the line are trained, kind, non-judgemental people who dedicate their time to helping others. One call could signal the start of you beginning to feel a little better.

Be Mindful AND *Hopeful*

With much emphasis these days on being 'in the moment' and thinking about the here and now, that might sometimes prove to be detrimental to your current situation. If life is hard, be it at home or school, and you are having a really bad day where you feel nobody understands you and you dislike yourself, it can be relaxing to pause and take in the world around you. Notice the birds, breathe slowly; feel calmer? Good. I have some great tips coming up for you. But what about practicality? What comes *after* you've calmed down?

To touch the surface lightly here, it can be extremely useful to have a bit of hope. Bad days do not equate to a bad life, and if there is one thing you can do to instil a little hope for tomorrow, then do it. It's what gets many people through the darkest of days; the thought that the sun will rise tomorrow can go some way to making you feel as though you've taken a bit of control over a thought that previously overwhelmed you.

You've Come A Long Way

In just one chapter, you've read quite a bit about this world we live in and you living in it. No longer is it a black and white world; many colours grace it, and everywhere you go, people like you will have or have asked the same questions you have in your mind.

They, like you, will have thought about what their gender identity means to them and how it affects their day-to-day life in precisely the same way.

Before I close this chapter off, in favour of two more that will really get you thinking about and understanding yourself even further, I want to touch on a subject that in no way intends to close you off from the rest of your journey.

To be bullied is to be misunderstood by someone who needs educating and who needs to learn respect. That is to say, it can happen to anybody, in any establishment, for any reason the bully deems acceptable (that doesn't mean the reason *is* acceptable).

Bullying is an unfortunate occurrence in many places, no matter who you are. A person can be bullied for how they dress, the type of bag they have, their likes, their hobbies, their glasses, their upbringing, their religion, their race, their gender, or how they identify. This list, sadly, is not exhaustive, and ***none*** of the reasons I have listed are an excuse to bully ***anyone.***

Have you ever been bullied? If you have, I wonder what the reason was and how it made you feel. Maybe in the past, you've been caught up in bullying, or witnessed it, and seen first-hand how it makes another person feel.

I was bullied at school for wearing braces. 'Brace Face,' 'Train Track,' and 'Metal Mouth' are just a few names that pop into my mind when I think about my experience of being at school with my fixed brace. It wasn't long before I thought, 'why did I even bother getting a brace in the first place if all people are going to do is call me names?'

I didn't think much about when the brace would be off, and I would have a dazzling, confident smile with straight teeth. Then, when I used to go to the orthodontist, he would ask me how it felt having it, and I would say uncomfortable, and he would remind me that 'it'll all be worth it in the end.'

If they are of the particular bullying trait, children, teenagers, and adults alike will find absolutely anything to pick on you for; you do not have to have gender identity curiosities or changes to fall, victim. I want you to remind yourself constantly of this because you, in your schools or colleges, will see it with your own eyes. It's uncomfortable, and you feel for that person. You wish they didn't have to go through it, but sadly, you cannot be exempt in life from what it throws at you, and that can be a real struggle for people, especially those experiencing gender changes.

Bullying now comes in so many forms, and it can be hard to escape how accessible we all are, as you read in my section about social media.

Examples you may have experienced or witnessed can include:

- Offensive jokes, language, mockery and innuendo.
- Insulting or abusive behaviour.
- Damage to property, such as lockers, bikes or your bag or coat.
- Graffiti
- Physical threats.
- Physical violence.
- Refusal to be kind or understanding because of a person's sexual orientation
- Refusal to be kind or understanding because of a person's gender identity.
- Deliberate exclusion from a conversation or professional or social activity.
- General intimidating behaviour.

Schools, like the rest of society, are establishments made up of people of all ages, each holding their individual values, opinions, and beliefs. These are all on their own spectrum, and some of these may be based on discriminative or prejudiced ideas.

Homophobia, transphobia, and biphobia are examples of such prejudice, but they are based on irrational and biased opinions that have the horrid ability to soak into our layers of skin, no matter how thick we think they are, and appear to us as ourselves being the problem.

We aren't.

You aren't.

Contemplation

You've worked your way through a hefty amount of the book already, and along the way, you've picked up language that may or may not be familiar to you. So as another world opens its door to you, and you take a step in and explore its surroundings, how does it make you feel?

Hopefully, as my intention was set out to do so, you are beginning to feel a little clearer about the thought process of your own gender identity, or even gender identity in general. But, of course, it isn't as easy as reading for a while and then having all the answers. Still, this initial chapter was intended to get you thinking a little bit further than previously and starting to look at your own life and environment and ask yourself how all those things help or hinder your journey.

As we progress into chapter two, more exercises begin, and ways to slow down the overwhelm will be given to you for those days you find particularly difficult to navigate. The beauty now is that you can flick back right to the beginning and re-read whatever you want, whenever you need to.

As ever, I encourage you to go at your own pace and ensure you feel comfortable, and if there is ever a time it feels too much, practise some breathing as we did before, and come back when you feel ready.

This is a safe place for you.

THREE

Exercises To Discover and Celebrate Who You Really Are

The previous chapter could have potentially left you feeling somewhat... frazzled. I don't expect you to breeze through the book without regularly checking in on yourself and ensuring you're feeling positive whilst reading through each section; I encourage it. This book, rather than for a fun and simple read, is more targeted at those of you who are feeling lost at the moment and who feel unable to see much light past the confusion. It, therefore, would be unfair not to incorporate some exercises that celebrate you.

This next chapter will help you get to know yourself better, hopefully making you feel more positive. Not only that, but you will be able to take the exercises with you wherever you go in life and make those difficult days a little less daunting. You might *feel* different, but you are you, which is something to celebrate.

I like to think of the world as one great big pick and mix. How fun would it be to have a massive tub of just cola bottles or jelly beans? When it's movie night, and you trundle off to the shop to treat yourself to a large pick and mix cup, do you fill it to the brim with the same sweet? I highly doubt it. Why not? One word... BORING!

The world is no different. At one point, though, we all want to fit in. We want to fit in because we don't want any negative attention brought towards ourselves, and I fully understand that. I remember being a teenager and wanting the same for myself. I hated football, yet found myself in a Liverpool shirt on numerous occasions, just because it was what people wore. Sounds so trivial, I know, but the essence of wanting to be universal to my peers was silent but very present.

The same could be said, on a very different level, for you. Can you think of anything you say or do or anything that you pretend to like in order to try and fit in? It could be liking a certain type of music, or clothing, or TV show, or how you style your hair, or even down to the way you laugh! We try our very best because we don't want the attention of being different.

Do any of you know or remember somebody at your school, or even in your neighbourhood, who is their own person, and who celebrates it? I was seventeen when I went to TopShop in Canterbury and fell in love with the most gorgeous pair of bright pink jeans with glitter on them. I want to take this time to remind you that this was at the peak of Britney Spears 'fame' days and that it could have been worse. Let me tell you, though, I stood in TopShop, and I held these jeans for what seemed an eternity. The only thing between holding them and owning them was the uncertainty of what wearing them could do for me, positively or negatively.

I didn't care.

I bought them and practically skipped home. I loved all things pink and sparkly, and after being raised with two older brothers where every week I would encounter a bruised knee or scratched elbow, and pretending to like Liverpool FC (sorry to all genuine fans, I'm sure they are fantastic, really), it was my time to shine and express myself.

Well, that lasted **a day.**

I wore them to school the day after I got them, and after the last bell of the day went, I proceeded to walk out of the school in the pouring rain. A girl in the year below was behind me and decided she would kick mud all up the back of me. She succeeded in this, coating my new jeans with huge, dark splats. I was mortified.

I went home and cried. All joking aside, the jeans may not have been everyone's cup of tea, and they were certainly different to what other kids my age were wearing at the time, but they were a simple expression of myself. I bought them, *knowing* I was taking a risk, but the desire to wear them outstripped the potential ridicule I'd endure in doing so.

Mum soaked them and got the mud out, and I thanked her. I didn't immediately wear them back to school, but I found I was able to wear them outside school, to the shops, the library, or around the house. It was only then that I thought about what happened and why.

You see, not everybody is ready when you are. Some people take a *really* flippin' long time to be ready for life or the acceptance of the decision of others, whatever those decisions may be. It's confusing when you have someone who tells you how fabulous you are or look and, on the other hand, have someone who literally flicks mud up your clothing for reasons I can only assume are deep-rooted jealousy.

I know it can seem a real contradiction to assume that a person who does that actually deep down loves your clothes or wants a pair themselves. So why not just say, 'hey, your jeans look amazing! Where did you get them?' instead of causing you pain and embarrassment, but it isn't that easy for so many people, but their reasons are never *you.*

Being raised in a house where it is deemed unacceptable to express your gender, sexuality or identity can leave a person resenting those who have that freedom to do so. That inner anger can turn outward when they see a person brave enough to push the boundaries and be happy and comfortable doing so. They may think, 'Why is she or he, or why are they allowed to do that, but not me?'

Now, For The Fun Part!

This book is a safe place for you to express who *you* are, no matter what your environment is. Maybe you're already pretty aware and confident about your identity, or maybe every thought is a first thought, and every action is pending. However you feel, and whatever your situation, we can work on it together.

Would you like to try some exercises now? If it isn't a good time for you currently, that's OK. Maybe you're reading on the train home or right before you go to bed after a long day. You're more than welcome to read through the exercises and come back to them at a better time for you.

I will start off with five questions that I'd like you to ask yourself about you. Remember, these are meant to celebrate you, not criticise you. So, if speaking highly or positively about yourself is new, go slow.

Go slow.

Not everybody finds it easy to point out the good or even work on the good parts because we become too fixated on our faults or what we think are hopeless traits within us. Equally, if our home environments aren't designed to celebrate us as the individuals that we are, we can become suppressed under the control or rules of those who are living unauthentically. Again, not your fault. Our parents or carers may be our family, but that doesn't mean they're right.

So – on that note, let's go ahead with the questions. Again, you can grab a pen and pad, or if you feel safer, you can use your mobile and type your answers in the Notes section.

Discover You

Question One: *In five words, describe your personality.*

This first question, like the others, has no right or wrong answers. One could write, 'I don't feel very confident,' or write a list of 5 separate words (that are allowed to contradict each other!) Sometimes it can be easier to not think too deeply about this one because then you're losing the flow of thought. Equally, if you look back at your words and decide you don't like them, try not to erase them and start again because those words, if you feel they genuinely describe you, are you.

I'm not asking for a perfect description, just an honest one. We've got the rest of the book to explore the more negative words you feel represent you.

To assure you, **here are mine:**

Procrastinator, caring, moany, worrier, funny.

Do you like my unique blend of *bleurgh* versus *wow, you're great!* Yes, this is life. I see the bad, I see the good, and they all make me, me. I try not to moan too much, but sometimes at night, when I go to use the toilet, and I sit down in pitch darkness on what should be a seat but is instead the ceramic because my delightful husband has left the seat up, yes, I have been known to moan.

Do any of yours make you chuckle in any way? If not, can you pick a negative one, if one exists on your list, and turn it into something you can laugh about? I bet you can find an example that shows this.

Question Two: *Who Inspires You?*

Inspiring people can come in all forms. It might be a parent or teacher. Potentially, and in this fantastic world filled with technological advances, you may be inspired by a YouTuber or TikTok star. Whoever they are, write them down, and then think about *why* they inspire you.

This is your answer, so it must come from the heart. Explore why and how they impact your life so positively. Maybe they have been through the emotional and confusing journey you are on now, and they've got many stories or affirmations that they share with their followers, with tips and advice on how to express yourself and that it's OK to do so.

Once you've done that, I would really like you to explore your answer a little deeper. I'd like you to think about, or possibly make notes, as to whether you are given this type of validation in your day-to-day life. For example, I am not in touch with my father. He isn't a very nice man, and to protect my own son from his behaviour, I made the decision to cut him from our life four years ago. But, on the other hand, I have a neighbour, who I will call Alan, who, since living in the house I'm in, has helped me with putting up some trellis in my garden, who knocked my rotting shed down for me, and who gives me DIY advice or support if I need it.

Those attributes are one of the reasons why I see Alan as a true friend. With unconditional support, no problem is too small for him; in return, I make him cake! He is only too happy to help, which is wonderful. So, the reason I find Alan a great role model is because he offers me something that I lack in my life, a father figure. Sometimes, we look to others for inspiration because it isn't on the table in our lives otherwise.

Maybe your inspirational person derives from the same place. What we lack in some ways, we gain in others. It's all about perception. However you got to your answers, it will tell you a little more about your life and the sort of people you want surrounding you. I call it the 'Golden Circle' – those people who fist pump you on the wins and walk with you during the hard times.

Would you like to emulate, or copy, some of your inspiration person's traits to others someday?

Question Three: *What do you like to do for fun?*

What a question – sure to lead to all kinds of diverse and beautiful answers from you! Those teenage years can lead to such an awesome blend of hobbies as well, so I will list a few that I think could crop up.

- *TikTok*
- *Gaming*
- *Being with friends*
- *Reading*
- *Watching Netflix*
- *Going to the cinema*
- *Singing in a band or playing an instrument*
- *Sports*
- *YouTubing*
- *Attending Sci-Fi conventions*
- *Playing with hair and make-up on various online tutorials.*

Now, for the second part of this question, I would like you to think about 3 things you'd really like to do for fun, but for whatever reason, you don't (yet). Is it about finding someone else to share your hobby or passion with you, or maybe you just need a little nudge in the right direction to get you started (and yes, you can nudge yourself!)

If these hobbies or 3 things guide you in any way to be able to express yourself further or get to know the person you want to be in finer detail, then the lists you are creating are going to go a long way in helping you discover how to get there.

Sometimes it can be uncomfortable thinking about things you'd like to do. It seems odd in itself that such a positive question could lead to a wide range of unsettling emotions, but hear me out. It can be possible to come from a place where your likes were not, or are not, validated.

Comments such as, 'God, you don't like this music, do you?' followed by a hearty scoff can see some people simply switch off the radio or streaming service. When applying make-up and enjoying experimenting with colours and contours, there may be similar responses. 'What on Earth do you look like?' As I write this, I feel cross. This is because I speak from experience, and I have had comments made towards me as a child and into my teenage and even adult years.

With every choice we make, we must own it. We must honour every passion that fires up our inner pit of desire. When someone constantly and consistently comes along with a massive bucket of water and douses those flames, that inner pit becomes damp and unable to withstand a spark, let alone a flame.

I recall that feeling well. I wonder if you do too.

Of course, it isn't like that for everybody, and I am certain there are many of you out there who feel lucky enough to be able to explore who you are, if not entirely, mostly. No matter the level of control other people feel they have over our likes or dislikes, it's important not to let go of them. Mostly though, if you can find out about those things that make you tick, then you can go some way to exploring them. If you aren't ready or are unsafe to do that at the moment, then in time, you will.

Discovering who you are and what you like is not a sprint. It is a marathon. One that doesn't time you out or makes you wear awkward fancy dress costumes (unless you want to, of course!), but one where you can appreciate the growth involved in growing. Miracles don't happen overnight, no matter how many movies contradict that idea. So if you wake up one morning and feel frustrated that things aren't moving as quickly as you'd like, or if you wonder why you don't feel a sense of wholeness, you should cut yourself some slack.

With every breath, you're figuring it all out, even if it doesn't appear that way to you.

Question Four: *What am I worried about?*

This list will be as long or as short as your personal circumstances allow. We all go through life coping in different ways, and your ways are not going to be invalidated here. However, worry can negatively impact our lives if we don't keep track of it. When events out of our control take us to places we'd rather not be; we can feel helpless, frustrated, and panicked.

As horrible as it is to worry, your body is reacting normally to your worries.

- *Trouble sleeping*
- *Lack of motivation*
- *Confusion or brain fog*
- *Tiredness*
- *Heart palpitations*
- *Sweating*
- *Overthinking*
- *Negative thoughts*
- *Saying 'no' to things that used to bring you joy*

These are all results of too much worry, and we often push them aside and say things like, 'well, that's just me, I don't sleep,' or, 'I'm tired, I don't really feel like it today,' or, 'No, I don't want to do that, what if something bad happens?'

It Doesn't Have To Be That Way

This part of the book encourages you to recognise the things that make your heart beat a little faster than usual or that make you retreat and say, 'not that, thanks!' At this stage, it's thinking and discovering. The next step is to act on those questions and find practical ways to reduce the worry you carry in your own life.

As stated before, a healthy amount of anxiety is actually good for us. Our brain wants to protect us from harm, so it sends lots of signals all over your body when you worry in order to protect it. Have you come face to face with a bear? Your heart will race and prepare you to run away. The problem occurs when there are no bears. Or if what used to be bears in the olden days are now bullies or the thought of starting your period, or your body is developing in ways that confuse you.

Maybe it could be the thought of having an honest conversation with a trusted other, whoever they may be. But, no matter how much you love them, there still may be a slight discomfort at the notion of opening up your most vulnerable self to another, especially when the reason you're opening up is *you*.

Worrying about revealing a new identity or expression is perfectly normal. No, it isn't a bear, but it is still scary, and the thought of having a conversation with somebody else about it may make you want to run far, far away. Included in the chaotic thoughts of the other person not responding well to your news, you might be worried about being teased, judged or ignored. There may even be questions directed towards you that you don't know yet how to answer.

Getting to know what worries you can give you a great insight into yourself and how you respond to those worries.

When we feel we don't have control over a situation, we panic. If we had a little insight into the reasons *why* it can be life-changing. With a little time and practical exercises that you'll see coming up, you'll be able to see the panic a mile off and respond to it before it has a chance to come for you.

Your worry list may only have a few points, or it may be a little longer, depending on who you are and what life you live. If your worries overwhelm you and make you feel like they are preventing you from living your normal day-to-day life, please make sure you speak to somebody. If there isn't a trusted adult in your life, then there are many avenues you can go down and many options you have.

Further into the book, you'll be given a list of charities and numbers specifically designed for *you*. You aren't a bother, and whatever you have to say, the people on the other end will have already heard from others thousands of times. Though you may feel alone, you most certainly are not, and your anxious thought process can find calming and soothing ways to reign the worry in.

Question Five: *What are my strengths?*

This is such a positive question and one that really gets you thinking about yourself. You could see your identity as a huge part of this question, or even the concept of you exploring it. Remember, if you feel it, write it. Nobody is going to pick up your list and laugh at it or tell you that you're wrong.

I do fully appreciate that if you are having a tough time, you may find answering this question really tricky. However, if you asked me twenty years ago to do the same, I would probably just stare at a blank piece of paper before finally writing some kind of list whilst looking over my shoulder to ensure my bully of a big brother wasn't peeking.

We live in a world now where a lot of people don't put themselves first. We have little brothers or sisters to look after, or we are in a rush to get to work or school, so we grab a snack bar instead of making time for a proper breakfast. We might stay up all night watching TV instead of revising for an exam or doing something more mundane in general but necessary. Self-care can go out the window if we are distracted, but believe it or not, writing answers to these questions is a form of self-care.

Long has it been a myth that to care for yourself, you must plaster your face in clay or take a nice bubble bath. Of course, these things are wonderful, but self-care goes deeper than that. Self-care means caring about yourself, and what better way than writing a list of all the things you see as your strengths.

Making sense of who you are and what you are great at is a bit like a zoom-out on a camera lens. Sometimes, when something is zoomed in, like one area of our lives that makes us feel lost or confused, we forget all the other great bits. Those bits that make us who we are, away from gender identity. You might be really good at following instructions when assembling something. That type of strength will have nothing to do with who you are and how you identify, but shining a light on it can give you the space you need to piece the 'you' that you are together.

Essentially, it is a question to make you feel less isolated. Feel free to incorporate your gender identity into the list; that would be fantastic. Maybe a strength is that you are proud of who you are becoming or the bravery it is taking you to explore gender identity as a whole.

If you have truly struggled with the last question and feel you can't think of one single thing, that's alright. What you can do for me is to work your way through the next section and try and figure out why it can feel difficult to celebrate a strength. It doesn't mean there's anything wrong with you; it just means you may have to dig a little deeper to find your confidence.

Next... The Practical!

Now you have worked your way nicely through five questions; I'd like you to start thinking about how the negative parts can assist you in your growth. I'm not at all insinuating that we all need to be perfect in order to be successful or live the life we desire, but it *is* important to be in a place where you can help yourself, should you need to.

That little toolbox I spoke about towards the start of the book will soon be armed with a few essentials, just for you.

There may come a time when you'll feel overwhelmed, and it may catch you off guard.

Here is a reminder of the questions to make it easier for you.

1. *In five words, describe your personality.*
2. *Who inspires you?*
3. *What do you do for fun?*
4. *What am I worried about?*
5. *What are my strengths?*

All questions have the ability to trigger you or make you think negative thoughts, and whilst this is not my intention, I want to make sure that those are addressed too, and any panic that crops up, or cropped up when you answered them, you can take some time to work on.

Some exercises may not involve a pen and paper, whilst others may. Once we have worked through these, I will talk a little bit about bodies and some exercises that can help us deal with the changes that you go through as a teenager. I want to do that separately because I feel it deserves a section all of itself.

Automatic Thoughts

When looking at your answers, which of them are negative? I would like you to pick one, just one for now. It doesn't have to be an entire answer; maybe it could be part of it. For example, one of the answers to the first question for me was that I procrastinate. I'm now going to use something called Cognitive Behavioural Therapy to change my answer into a more positive one.

Cognitive Behavioural Therapy (or CBT) is a concept therapists use (in fact, anyone can use) that turns negative thoughts or feelings around, allowing you to explore them and create new thoughts are that more helpful going forward. It is a good method used for people who have anxiety or depression and can be life-changing.

CBT has been shown to be an effective treatment for children and teenagers because it responds positively to stressful thoughts and situations. It really tackles that feeling of not being good enough or having general low self-esteem, and the best part is, because it is a really practical tool, you can start to notice differences within yourself quite quickly.

So, I will take my procrastination answer, and explain how this practical exercise works, so that you can copy the method wherever you are.

Trigger – I get frustrated when I keep putting things off.

Automatic thought – 'Things aren't getting done because I keep wasting time doing nothing. I scroll my social media accounts or play Roblox (yes, I actually do).

New thought – It's OK to take breaks from work or studying. I will make sure I create set times to relax and create alarms for when it is time to do some work.

It didn't take me long to explore why I procrastinate, and although I still do it, I have gotten much better at realising I do it. Procrastination is a form of self-sabotage. We do it because we can become overwhelmed with our tasks or because we are doing very well, and our mind is entering a space that reflects that. We can actually hold ourselves back by procrastinating, and it is to gain control of situations that make us uncomfortable.

What about you? What words may you have used, or what have you written for what worries you? Give a good example, such as, 'I worry that if I don't sleep well, I'll not wake up in time for school and miss that important test. Then I will not get a good grade, my parents will be angry with me, and ultimately, I will fail school.' These are what are known as catastrophic thoughts or catastrophising. At 2 am, there isn't much room for rational thoughts when we get so caught up in one bad thought that leads to a bad life we have created in our minds and convinced it that it's all true.

Have you ever been through something like that before? It's incredibly frustrating, isn't it? So soon, something as simple as going to bed can instil so much worry, and soon your bed will be your biggest enemy, no matter how much lavender you sprinkle on it.

Getting to the bottom of the problem, or finding the root cause, is something that can help. If sleep is an issue for you, and you find you struggle on school nights, you might like to think about what worries you the most about being at school. If you are confused about your gender identity, it could be that you struggle to sleep the most on the nights before PE because you know you have to get changed amongst those who match the gender they were born with.

This can be extremely uncomfortable, especially if you know someone, or have yourself, been teased for the way they or you look.

Automatic thoughts can help in so many different areas of your life, and their main aim is to change how you perceive the world according to your beliefs or what has been expected of you. They are a little bit like self-talk – that voice in your head. The thoughts themselves cannot be controlled, but how we deal with them can be, with practice.

With a bit of time, you can think more productively, but mostly, you can squash your distorted thoughts and respond to them with this new superpower!

Celebrate Your New Thought Process!

When it comes to celebrating who we are, these wonderful new thought processes are:

Empowering
A form of self-acceptance
A form of gratitude

Fact or Opinion?

This is a really thought-provoking exercise, and you can do it on paper, on screen or in your mind. As long as you pause to question your thought or belief and try to dissect where it is coming from, you're onto a winner!

Fact or opinion is another CBT-based process where you make a statement and decide whether it is... you guessed it – fact or fiction. This is very evidence-based; for example, it is a fact that the sky is blue. It isn't a case of opinion; once the clouds are stripped away, the sky is *always* blue. It can be an opinion that the weather is beautiful, but the sky itself isn't up for debate.

With CBT, it is important to separate facts from opinions. If you treat an opinion such as, 'I am a horrible person,' as a fact, it can contribute to depression, anxiety, and/or other problems. What you'd be doing is giving yourself more reasons to feel sad or worried about when the truth could be far from what you perceive to be true.

Sometimes it is possible for a small fact to turn into an overall opinion. For example, 'I had an argument with my best friend' could lead to the opinion, 'My best friend hates me.' What I am suggesting you do, is spot the difference between fact and opinion because it can challenge irrational beliefs. As soon as you start to erase an opinion you once held down as a belief, then the power of belief can also be erased. This is like a **brand new way of life.**

Can you think of a statement right now that you could challenge and realise is actually an opinion? It has to be something strong, something that stops you from doing what you like in life, or something that makes you feel anxious or sad.

I will think of a statement now.

I feel quite tired today.

I know this to be a fact because I was up early for the sunrise during yesterday's Summer Solstice, as I do every year, so it always takes me a few days to recharge!

What about this one?

I am ugly.

Is that fact or opinion? What would make it a fact? Is there an official beauty scale we all adhere to in life, similar to a law? No, there is not.

Being ugly would really be my own opinion (if I thought it were true) and would be a root cause of why I may not dress confidently or go to many social events. The opinion itself is damaging, but also the consequences of the opinion can equally be terrible for my mental health. For example, I could avoid wearing certain clothes and refuse to go out and see my friends all because I am too concerned about how ugly I think I am.

Gender identity can come into play here too. Can you think of any statements that revolve around gender identity and decide if they are facts or opinions? I'll have a go.

- ***I am ugly (a universal statement!).***
- ***I don't know what to wear.***
- ***My parents will hate me if I decided to transition.***
- ***I am unsure how to express myself.***
- ***Other people won't like me if I identify differently.***
- ***I will be bullied at school if my new identity is revealed.***
- ***My teacher uses 'them/they' pronouns.***

What do you think about those statements? Some of them might be pretty hard to read, as they may be relevant to you. But, no matter how hard they were to read through, was each question fact or opinion? Saying your parents will hate you if you decide to transition is a strong belief that a certain outcome will be true, but it can't be a fact because you don't know what will happen in the future. Hate is also a very strong word. Your parents may well be surprised, and that's OK. It's a huge thing to hear, but being surprised is in no way linked directly to a feeling of hate. That's just the part you've made up because you feel scared.

On another note, let's look at the teacher's comment. If they use pronouns such as them or they, it means that is how they wish to identify. It's different, but it's out there, and everyone knows. They are comfortable being who they are and celebrate it by simply being themselves. How would that make you feel if someone you knew had already changed their pronouns? Relief? Inspiration? The feeling that you aren't alone? All those thoughts are *good* thoughts. They are there to give you hope that you too can be whoever you feel you are and that it'll be OK.

I wonder if you can see facts and opinions a little clearer now and are able to see the difference between them. Perhaps you could do that to help you when you have a worry or sad thought that takes you away from the moment.

When you feel overwhelmed, pause, step back and assess what's really going on.

Is this fact or opinion?

If it is an opinion, where does that come from? Low self-esteem? Overhearing someone else say it about another person? The reluctance to allow the fact to speak for itself?

With practice, you can better spot the difference between fact and opinion. This will really help you in your journey.

Home House Points

You're all familiar with how house points work. For every good thing you do at school, there is a chance you may have received a house point, or at least have heard of them and how they operate.

Home House Points is something you can do yourself, and with every question written, you can give yourself a Home House Point for every **yes**. There are 14 questions in total. This exercise aims to understand that sometimes it can be challenging to celebrate who we are because of our environments.

If bigging yourself up or picking out all the good parts doesn't come naturally, there isn't anything wrong with that or you. In fact, the thought of discovering your identity may make you uncomfortable because certain aspects of your life have led you to *believe* you should feel uncomfortable, but the reality is very different.

Let's start with the questions. Remember, every *yes*, give yourself a point.

1. *Are you a carer for a parent or sibling in your house?*
2. *Are you, or have you ever been in foster care?*
3. *Have you got a parent with an addiction (gambling, drugs, alcohol etc.)?*
4. *Do you have an absent parent?*
5. *Do you have a parent who is abusive, either physically or emotionally?*
6. *Do you feel safe and secure in your home?*

7. *Do you come from a religious home?*
8. *Are you of an ethnic minority?*
9. *Do you have a good relationship with your parents?*
10. *If you have siblings, do you get on with them?*
11. *Do you feel your parents push you too much?*
12. *Do you do well in school?*
13. *Have you got at least one good friend?*
14. *Do you look back on your childhood with happy memories?*

Now, count up your scores.

These House Points don't work the same way they do at your school, or if you have heard of them. These House Points are like little indicators that stress or sadness/worry will be more common in your life the higher your score is. There isn't a threshold or a cut-off point for scores above or below a certain number, but the questions are designed to look at what you answered *yes* to and think about how that affects you celebrating who you are.

Your life outside your identity will play a big part in how gender identity, or the discovery of it, can affect you and how you celebrate yourself. Sometimes we fail to see that even the most negative experiences are worth celebrating because we survive them and use them to be stronger people. Let's break down the questions, and I will explain a little about them.

Are you a carer for a parent or sibling in your house?

This is important to think about, not to encourage resentment for looking after a loved one, but to think about how much time you have to consider yourself. Being a home carer can mean long hours and ensuring you put someone else before you much of the time. Home carers do not get the recognition they deserve; if you are one, you will know how hard you work and how you forget your own priorities for a great deal of the time.

You learn not to put yourself first when at times, you need to.

Are you, or have you ever been in foster care?

I don't need to explain to you how chaotic and scary it is to move from house to house without ever feeling it's your home. If you are or have been in the care system, you will know that familiar feeling that nobody loves you or cares about you.

This can lead to a really low view of yourself or that things are never going to get better. You may feel anger and frustration at your situation or jealousy towards those who seem to have it all with a permanent residence.

It can also lead to a lack of people you can trust or feel you can turn to if you need to have a discussion about your identity, and that can leave you feeling incredibly lonely.

Have you got a parent with an addiction?

Watching someone, you love appear helpless to their struggles can lead to many consequences. Masking your own issues surrounding it by imitation is one, and that is the hardest to undo. Mostly, the stresses and anxiety that surround the inconsistency of your parent can lead to destruction within the home, and if you live there, then that can include you.

If a parent is forever caught up in their own problems, you could wonder if they'd ever have time to listen to you and your gender identity questions you might want to share with them. But unfortunately, that would make it extremely hard to approach them for support.

Do you have an absent parent?

Having an absent parent doesn't necessarily mean you will lose out in any way. On the contrary, being raised by a mother or father alone can often forge a lovely bond between you both. However, it can sometimes leave us wondering why they aren't around and if they chose not to be. I know several people who have taken it quite personally if their mum or dad is not in their lives through any other reason than death and have struggled to maintain relationships with mother or father figures of the same gender.

When we need that type of attention the most, it is not there, and it can hurt and be confusing. 'What have I done wrong?' 'What's so terrible about me?' These, amongst many others, are some of the questions you might ask yourself, and as you enter this pivotal part of your life, where you need support now more than ever, there is just a gap where that parent should be.

It can affect your journey, but it shouldn't define it.

Do you have a parent who is abusive, either physically or emotionally?

This is something so many people relate to, and remember, there are so many different types of abuse, but they all count as abuse. There isn't one form less likely to damage you than another; they all hurt and shouldn't happen. But, sadly, for many, they do.

When you go through body changes or inner turmoil related to your gender identity, you're unlikely to find the support you need from an abusive parent. You are already going to be aware of the consequences of speaking up about yourself and are likely going not to want to do so for fear of triggering another abusive episode.

So what do you do?

You're likely to struggle in silence.

You shouldn't, but you do.

At the end of the book, when I list the support available, you'll find an extensive amount of help for you if you have been or are being abused by a parent.

Your home is somewhere where you should feel safe, and if you don't, you're not having all your needs met. This leads nicely into the next question.

Do you feel safe and secure in your own home?

If you do, then let me be the first to tell you how happy that makes me. We take the safety of our home for granted and assume it is only compromised if a burglary were to take place. A stranger could take our possessions and treasures, and our home would never feel the same again. We might even be afraid to be there alone if they returned. What about everyday life?

Feeling unsafe at home can come from the feeling of being neglected, parents working long hours and leaving you home alone, parents who are more interested in their own needs than yours, or parents bringing frequent friends or changing partners home with them in your presence. But, of course, the list is not exhaustive and can go on and on, and perhaps you can think of your own reasons why you may not feel safe in your home.

When we don't feel safe, we retreat. We retreat to a place where we *do* feel as safe as possible, but it's unlikely to be enough.

If loneliness is a big part of you not feeling safe, then you may rely on inappropriate things to keep you company, such as talking with strangers online. Unfortunately, this isn't a safe way to explore yourself and discover things about yourself on this journey because your age makes you vulnerable to all kinds of motives.

Do you come from a religious home?

Religion can play a significant role in how people respond to the concept of gender identity. For example, it is forbidden to be gay without punishment in some cultures. This happens on this very day in certain parts of the world, and I have yet to fathom how this is at all possible.

If you come from a home of religion that you know would affect your chances of identifying differently in a positive way, then you're bound to be scared. This can stop you from wanting to celebrate who you are because of the beliefs that come from your home. Whilst you may share their religion, you may disagree with some of the rules, especially as they directly affect you, the real you.

Are you of an ethnic minority?

If you are from a background of an ethnic minority, you already know what it is like to be the minority, and whilst more and more people are discovering they can identify in different ways, they still sit in the minority of society.

Whilst these minorities may differ, they effectively mean one thing.

There is an uphill climb for **justice**.

Luckily, we live in this amazing world, where there are celebrations in the name of everybody every day: Black

History Month, and Pride Month, to name a few. So, society *is* getting better, but the climb is still uphill.

Do not let who you are or where you're from dictate the level of celebration you should give yourself.

Do you have a good relationship with your parents?

Those with a strong relationship with their parents are more likely to feel the need to express the celebration of who they are. Leadership and direction from an early age are very helpful in clear and confident journeys of exploration.

I must add that even children or teenagers with the strongest bond with their parents can feel anxious about speaking honestly about their gender identity. Ultimately, they may get along like a house on fire, but their opinions may differ on what gender identity means to them. Some people think it's a 'phase,' which belittles the person going through changes.

This has no reflection on you – and you should continue celebrating who you are regardless of what other people may think.

If you have siblings, do you get on with them?

If you have a sibling that you're close with, this is a great starting point to be able to confide in a trusted other, particularly if they are older than you and can guide and support you. We take siblings for granted, and yes, we all bicker, but generally, if you have kind and close siblings, you can be sure they will be there for you.

Some of us aren't lucky to have nice siblings or even be in touch with them. This is the case for me. With 2 brothers, I am close to one, and I never see the other. I'm OK with that because I can talk to one about anything, and vice versa. It may be similar for you.

If you don't have siblings, that doesn't matter. It simply means you may have alternative family members, like a cool aunt or uncle, to speak to. Of course, some of you may not but don't fret. Remember, you're never alone, not when there are so many charities out there ready for your call.

Do you feel your parents push you too much?

It's easy to feel pressured by parents. They can sometimes think they want the best for you, and instead of that encouraging feeling you get, you feel like you're being cornered in a small room, and the stress levels inside you can rise.

Sometimes when we feel stressed, we run the other way. So if you feel like doing that sometimes, it's OK. Most behaviours can be explained and worked on, as we did above, with automatic thoughts or fact vs opinion.

Do you do well in school?

Learning doesn't come naturally to us all. In fact, so many people thrive when given practical tasks to do, such as putting a car engine together or grooming a horse. We aren't all destined to stick our noses in books and be the next top lawyer, and that's OK. I wonder how well you do at school.

If you really thought about it, do you cruise along alright but have that one subject you absolutely love/loathe? For me, I used to **hate** science with a passion, but I did really well in and enjoyed English. However, since leaving school over 20 years ago, I have taken a keen interest in science, particularly astronomy.

If you do well in school, you can celebrate that about yourself and think about how great you feel there. This may help you when you do decide to out your gender identity because you'll feel more positive about being there.

If school isn't for you, the good news is it doesn't last forever! It might appear that way when you walk into double maths on a Monday morning, but I assure you, the world is waiting for you, and soon enough, you'll be partaking in it.

Have you got at least one good friend?

Some of us are luckier than others when it comes to friends, but it isn't about quantity. If you have at least one good friend in your life, then you know you've got one person who will be on your side. That in itself is something to celebrate about you.

Thinking about it, they are friends with you because you're a cool person, and changing your identity is drastically unlikely to change that.

If you are low on friends or trusted others, this can be something you can think about. We all have the ability to make friends, although it can be really difficult if it isn't something we can do naturally. How about thinking of ways you could meet small groups of people, such as a club or an in-school group that takes your interest?

Do you look back on your childhood with happy memories?

This last question is really thought-provoking. Of course, your childhood will be a lot fresher in your mind than mine, but thinking about it will give you a reason to celebrate the person you've become.

Have you been through many things and can stand up and tell your story? Has your life been pleasant, loving and easy?

Have you had repeated trauma in your life that has left you feeling petrified about the topic of gender identity? There is no right or wrong, but regardless of your history, you are here right now, reading something that is ***helping*** you. You've taken the time to support your choices, and that alone should be **celebrated.**

Self-Celebration!

Now you have spent a little time working through the processes and exercises that discover and celebrate who you are; it is time to reflect on what self-celebration actually is, just to give you a gentle reminder.

Celebrating who you are right now, not who you wish you were or who you may be in the future
Learning to love and accept the parts of yourself you don't like or struggle with
Working out what you would like to do and making sure you do it more
Your own personal celebration of yourself, as private or public as you'd like
A tool of support for you to have ready at all times
Your own secret weapon!

Remember why you're doing this. Your goal is to explore yourself and who you are right now. It isn't an invite to be a person less awesome than you currently are, so you should remember to use your toolbox for the greater good.

What Self-Celebration is NOT

A form of attention-seeking behaviour
Proving you're better than someone else
Bragging
Being mean or a bully
Proving your worth to other people
Celebrating irresponsibly with alcohol or other substances

Diary / Journaling

Some people really respond well to keeping a type of diary or journal. These can be virtual or in paper form; there's no right or wrong. You may even prefer to make voice notes on your phone, so you can record as you walk to or from school.

Diaries, or journals, are great for writing down worries or fears because it can feel like you are plucking them from your mind and getting them in a place where you can make more sense of them. Sometimes, if I have a worry, I write it down on my laptop in a special folder I have. I write the date and tap away until I feel lighter and my head feels a little clearer.

Writing in a diary or journaling doesn't have to be a daily thing. You may feel you need to dip into it at certain times more than others, and that's OK. You have to do what works for you. Doing it in some way is very therapeutic, though, and as you look back on difficult times, you'll remember how you felt and how you dealt with it. They are great reflective tools, and I do recommend you start one if you feel it would be beneficial.

It could be something that makes a huge difference in how chaotic it can feel when you think about your gender identity. But, so often, it's never one big thing we do to feel better, it's lots of little things, and this idea is a powerful contender for positive change.

If you wanted to start journaling, which format would work best for you?

Ways To Ground and Be Yourself Authentically

When the world gets a little crazy, we can neglect our needs. When we have busy days, or stressful periods in our lives, the most helpful thing to do, is pause. In what ways do you like to pause?

Yoga

I like to practise yoga. I'm not an expert at it, but there are several stretches or holds that really relax me, and each time I take even just 15 minutes out of my day to make time for it, I notice the difference. Silly as it sounds, that is something to celebrate about myself because I recognise when my body and mind need a time out.

As your own body goes through changes, or you are on the cusp of believing it needs to physically change for you to identify comfortably, you might feel confusing thoughts about it or how you look. Yoga is universal, and it focuses on the body in terms of strength and flexibility. It is good for anybody, whether it's one you like or not, and ultimately is a gentle and kind way for you to celebrate the vessel that has carried you and taken care of you. As it changes, yoga can still be with you and help you.

Be Outside

A simple stroll outside can make all the difference. If you're stuck in a rut and can't manage to go for a walk, then the act of being outdoors is a great place to start. Feeling the fresh air or the sun on your face is a natural mood booster and can lift your happy hormones. You might not think it, but you are doing something for yourself, and all these little things help give you the incentive to celebrate you.

I like to be in my garden barefoot a lot, so my feet can sink into the grass. It makes me feel connected to something bigger than me, and my worries immediately feel smaller, even temporarily. I know your problems may not go away just by standing on the grass barefoot, but if practised enough, it could start to give you a renewed sense of purpose.

Mindfulness

Do you hear that word all the time? Mindfulness is a word that so many people use nowadays, and how they use it can vary so much.

Mindfulness can be practised however you feel comfortable doing so. It is the ability to be fully present, in the moment, and being aware of what we are doing without being overly reactive or overwhelmed. Sounds like a lot, right? It may seem that way at first, but actually, it's about breaking down all the big things going on into smaller, more manageable pieces. As you do this, your sense of power can build your confidence and lower your stress.

That is something to celebrate.

It can be something as simple as eating. When you take a huge bite of your favourite meal, really take the time to smell, taste and truly enjoy it. Chew a little slower and discover all the flavours. Think about how happy you feel, and live in the moment.

What about a walk? If you usually stroll the streets, phone in hand, and head buried into your screen, try putting it in your pocket, even for part of the walk. Lift your head and look around. Look up at the sky, watch the clouds, or listen to the birds or leaves rustling. This is a refreshing way to feel gratitude and hope for today. Doing this regularly will help you untangle any current confusion you may feel about yourself because you're developing more tools to stop, pause, and breathe.

Remember

There are no exercises here that are suited more to those who identify as male, female, non-binary, transgender, asexual, or any other form of identity. They are simple and effective ways to develop your thoughts and feelings through any transition you may be going through or are thinking of going through.

Like all exercises, they will make you stronger, but these are to purely make your mind stronger, which will, in turn, give you a much-needed confidence boost and allow you to realise that although things seem confusing right now, they won't always be.

There will be ways in which you use these exercises, and they will differ from person to person.

Top Tips For Doing These Exercises Yourself!

1. *Take your time. There really is no rush.*
2. *Try to do them in a safe place, so you feel at your most comfortable.*
3. *Relax. You shouldn't feel pressure.*
4. *If you feel stuck or not ready, come back to them another time.*
5. *If you find one exercise you enjoy in particular and the rest tricky, that's OK.*
6. *Take them with you in your day-to-day life – you'll find you could use them often.*
7. *If you do decide to keep a diary, make sure it is in a safe place.*

Contemplation

All those thoughts and exercises have hopefully carried you a little further into your journey of self-discovery. The aim of those exercises, in particular, is to provide you with ongoing support. I don't believe they can only be done once, so your answers may surprise you when you're having a rough day and feel low. That's when you can use the fact or fiction question and decide if it's your self-doubt talking.

You may, at times, have felt a little discomfort as you manoeuvre new grounds and find yourself thinking in new ways that are unfamiliar to you. Despite the positive changes you're making in thinking about what gender identity means to you, there are likely to be still emotions going on that you've never felt before.

However you decide to carry on with these exercises, or whether or not you decide journaling is for you, I have every faith you will pick and choose ideas that work for you personally, which is what matters.

Have you thought about how brilliant you are today? As you sit and read these words this very moment, how about taking one final moment before the chapter ends with thinking about yourself in general. Nothing in particular, and nothing that might make your ego become problematic, but just a general high five to yourself.

It seems odd to think about high-fiving yourself, doesn't it? Mostly because it might feel awkward. But why do we high-five others? Because we are celebrating them, and they are accepting it from you. It could be a scored goal, a job well done, or a simple,' hi, how are you?' to a friend.

You're sorting through your thoughts, working out how to make your mind a more positive place, figuring out who you are, accepting that it may not be a perfect road, but the road is yours nonetheless, as well as creating a safe space for yourself. You deserve a high five!

Is it time you gave yourself a high five?

The next chapter will pick apart some questions and answers you may have or that are common with people your age and going through the same as you. The chapter aims to be reassuring and offer you ways to think about your own life.

Ready When You Are!

FOUR

Q&A and Resources

So here we are, the final chapter! How are you feeling, having read through a large amount of information, experiences and tips? It's likely been a unique blend of information and feelings of hope; at least, I would hope so.

As I continue to help you find your way in this chaotic world and reassure you that your gender identity is something to be celebrated and not hidden, I wanted to end the book with a number of questions that you may have circling in your mind, that you may not feel like asking somebody.

It's natural to have questions, and you may have some that aren't listed. If that's the case, I encourage you to explore them using the new tools you have learned and find ways to point you in the right direction. The answer may be within you already, and with all this newfound wisdom, you could find that they appear clearly!

I promised you a plethora of resources that can help you if you need support and a list of some social media people to whom you may relate. In addition, I've endeavoured to offer you responsible pages with positive messages for you during this time. Of course, it's easy to find negativity online, but my advice would be to steer clear.

Negativity is a bit like a common cold. Once it sneezes on you, it will likely affect you in some way and make you feel pretty rubbish. Well, these resources will be like a nice hot cup of honey and lemon, with the intention to make you feel good, and feel a little clearer about those topics you might be struggling with.

You'll find them right at the end, and I hope you gain something from them, even if it is the knowledge that help and support are just a click or call away.

Before we get there, let's take a look at some common questions people in your shoes may have. Remember – try not to feel embarrassed. We are all human, and we all have the same thoughts and worries from time to time.

The aim of these questions is really to be an open page for you to be able to explore the topics that may seem tricky to navigate or that you are too embarrassed to ask somebody else.

They aren't designed to pressure you or make you feel silly. I firmly believe there is no such thing as a silly question, especially when it comes to gender identity, as there is so much to learn.

The Questions

Why do some people identify as non-binary, transgender or any other identity that is different from simply 'male' or 'female'?

To be a **non-binary** person is exactly what it sounds like. It is the existence of yourself and your identity outside the binary definitions of 'man' or 'woman,' or masculine and feminine.

Often when asked, non-binary people I know or have spoken to say that a definitive gender identity is something that simply doesn't make sense to them. A popular thought is that many identities and expressions can exist within the definition of non-binary, and that is why so many people feel so comfortable identifying that way.

To be non-binary can be as simple as deciding to live a life as true to oneself and free as possible. Individually though, it can mean something much more personal. This can mean changing names, pronouns, wardrobes, or maybe even nothing at all. The important factor is that they feel they are being true to themselves.

When non-binary people identify that way, and when asked about their own gender, they say, 'I am **me-gender**.' Being yourself is powerful but also vulnerable despite any parts you were born with or how society views you. It is, however, a huge statement to society that says people can be more than what they were merely told to be.

Transgender is another way to identify, and many people do. There is more information in the upcoming question.

Changing the way you identify can feel like coming home. To others, it may seem confusing. They may ask you why you wish to identify differently, and it can be challenging to explain to somebody who you truly are, but the one important factor to remember is that you are honouring the real you.

So many more people, not just teenagers your age, no longer look at the human body as something that starts and ends with what they were born with. Instead, female or male body parts are seen as mere **bodies,** and that view isn't based simply on sex or gender.

It is empowering to think this way and identify in a way that makes you feel more you, and even adults, go through this thought process too, which is why more and more people identifying differently is increasing.

What does it mean to be transgender, and how does it work?

Transgender people have a gender identity that is different from the gender they were born with. *'Trans'* is often used as an abbreviation.

When we are born, a doctor usually says we are male or female based on what our bodies look like. Most people who were labelled men at birth continue to identify that way, and the same goes for women. However, some people's gender identity – that feeling of who they truly are – is different from what was initially expected when they were born.

A transgender woman lives as a woman today but was thought to be male when she was born. A transgender male lives as a man today but was thought to be female when he was born. Some transgender people actually identify as neither female nor male but as a combination of both.

People can realise they are transgender at any age. It is that awareness, that first memory, where they just know. It could be that they feel they don't fit in without fully understanding why, which can happen at a very young age. People who feel this way might try and avoid thinking or talking about their gender out of fear, confusion or shame. That might sound familiar to you.

Trying to repress your gender identity or even change what your heart is trying to tell you doesn't work and can be very damaging to a person's emotional and mental health. More people are now coming forward and are able to name and understand their own feelings and experiences and, as a result, feel safer sharing them with others.

Recognising who they are and deciding to start gender transition is a huge step for anybody in that position. So much reflection often takes place, and transgender people risk social stigma, discrimination and harassment when they tell others who they really are. Just as accepting as parents, friends or people you work with may be, they are just as likely not to be, and that fear can run through a person who has all this going on in their world.

Despite all this, there is nothing more life-affirming and even life-saving than being yourself. Imagine for a moment *not* being you, on a very deep level, day in, day out. Living that type of lie is incredibly detrimental to your health and adds to the false expectations of other people in your life.

Medical Treatments

Some, but not all, transgender people undergo medical treatments to make their bodies match more with their gender identity and help them live healthier lives. Of course, not everybody wants or asks for this, but it can be critical for others.

People ultimately should make decisions about their bodies based on their individual needs. Medical procedures can include:

1. Hair removal or growth treatments
2. Hormone therapy
3. Various surgeries to make their face, anatomy and chest more in line with their gender identity

These options are not taken lightly, and they do not happen and are not planned overnight. It takes time to be able to have these procedures, and at your age, you may not be thinking that far ahead. Depending on how long you've had your thoughts, you also might be. This is something you can initially talk to your parents or carers about and go from there.

How does someone who has gone through a transition with their gender identity date?

Dating as a teenager can be a minefield. With hormones racing, lots of people to discover and get to know, all the while dealing with school and bodily changes is so much to deal with at one moment in time.

Is there more anxiety for those who change their gender identity?

Yes – and more!

Of course, there is going to be more anxiety when it comes to dating if you identify differently from what society has accepted as the mainstream identities. You'll probably wonder what other people will think of your decision, and there will be natural questions such as who will you be attracted to, or how will you go about expressing your interest in another person?

These questions, when presented to someone who identifies in alignment with their birth gender assignments, can be daunting. They can be even more so if you are still figuring yourself and your own unique identity out, but that should never stop you from dating or taking chances with people you like.

Personally speaking, I am female with female body parts; I was born that way, and I identify that way. I have had my heart broken, really broken, twice. The first time was with the first boy I loved. We were together for over five years, and one day, he just decided he outgrew me and our relationship. I don't think I left the house for weeks, and I thought I would never love again.

I did, but he wasn't ready for all the emotions that came with a relationship. To my knowledge, he is still single, but he broke my heart when he rejected me. I found love a third time with my current partner, and we have a son together. We have been together for over ten years, and let me tell you, at times, he can really grate my garlic, but that is love. I found it after heartache, and you, too, will find love.

If it hurts, you know it was real. And if it doesn't work out, have faith that you will be given another opportunity to love in your life.

Your gender identity has nothing to do with love. Love is love. You'll hear that a lot, by the way, because it is relevant, regardless of how you identify and who you love.

Putting yourself out there and dating, whether you're transgender, non-binary, straight, gay or bisexual, it is ***imperative*** that you know how possible it is to have happy, fulfilling relationships, no matter your gender identity or sexual orientation. So let's have a look at things to keep in mind when it comes to dating through a transition.

Share Your Identity

If you're getting to know someone that you may end up going on a date with, you may want to let them know your gender identity or how you hope to transition. It's ultimately up to you when and how you do this, if at all. It might be that you are upfront from the beginning and place all your cards on the table. On the other hand, you may prefer to get to know the person better to get a better sense of them before bringing the subject up. It's always important to remember that you only need to share what information you feel comfortable doing so. Nobody is or should be rushing you.

Staying Safe Online

The internet can be a great place to meet like-minded people, and for the majority, it works really well in keeping people connected and talking. It is fantastic for support groups because teenagers the world over, just like you, want to find or build their own community so that they feel included in this journey.

You should remember a few basic rules about meeting people online. First, always be careful not to share personal information such as where you live or where you go to school or college, or anything else about you that you'd rather keep quiet.

Make sure you reach a point of mutual trust before you give your number to anyone, and by mutual trust, you must **both** feel comfortable. Some people are not who they claim to be online, and there are untold stories about people as young as you meeting up with someone they met online, only to come in harm's way. If you think it won't be you, I'm positive they thought the same about themselves. These are rare occasions, but they happen and continue to happen.

Meeting People

Finding ways to meet new people can be a challenge in the dating world for anyone. Joining groups and attending events can help you and be a great way to meet people who like the same things you do. These don't have to be LGBTQA+ or non-binary-focused groups, but spending time within those circles can give you the opportunity you need to meet like-minded people and add to your understanding of what you're going through and your experiences.

Clubs or societies within schools and colleges can open many doors for social interaction as well and could lead to getting to know someone in a natural environment that you may end up going on a date with.

Having Clear Boundaries

First – let's get one thing clear. Boundaries are important in life, in ALL walks of life, whether or not you are dating, working, young, old, black, white, bisexual or transgender.

Setting a boundary means deciding what **you** are comfortable with and communicating it to the person you are dating. It even extends to family, friends and work colleagues, but in this instance, these boundaries could be sexual, physical or emotional.

You might think of some others, but for me, my first thoughts are how much time you spend together or what types of questions or conversations you feel comfortable having with your date.

Expect some questions from your date if they want to know more about your experience or thoughts on gender identity. General interests can lead to insightful conversations, but only if you feel comfortable having them.

You get to decide your boundaries, and if they are not respected, then letting them know you cannot continue to see them is a strong way to maintain those boundaries.

Respectful Dating

You should be respected, in any relationship, as everyone else should as well. Your gender identity should be accepted, validated and celebrated whilst dating, so your partner should refer to you with your correct name or pronouns.

Taking A Break

It isn't easy to date, so it is important to look after yourself. Remember that it's okay to take time out from meeting new people whenever you need to, especially if school is busy, as your work is so important to your future. Taking a break doesn't mean you won't find someone at another point if you want to, but it can really make you turn your focus inward and look after yourself sometimes.

Don't Forget The Other Stuff

Even if you want to spend every waking moment with your partner, don't forget your friends, and continue to make time for your hobbies too.

If Your Gender Identity Is Not Accepted By Your Date

A huge part of being in a relationship is accepting and being accepting of who one another is, regardless of your gender identity. Everyone deserves this, and sharing your gender identity is a sign of trust, which is a big step.

If hearing your news is unexpected in some way to them, that isn't an excuse for insensitive or abusive reactions. If this is the case, removing yourself from that situation is okay.

This can be incredibly difficult to experience, so it is essential you seek support from someone, whether it's someone you know or a contact at the end of the book. Don't be alone.

Remember

Dating can be very exciting, but it can also sometimes hurt when a person you like doesn't like you back. The important thing to remember is to remain true to yourself and your own values at all times. There isn't room to re-model yourself based on what somebody else wants from you. Life is too short to live it to make others happy, and that includes dating.

There will be a time when you'll meet someone who accepts you for being you, with no compromise.

How would you start a difficult conversation with someone about your gender identity?

Does the thought currently bring you out in a bit of a sweaty panic? Your heart might skip a beat or start racing because once you've said it, it leads the way to a host of questions and conversations over time.

Your initial thought, though, is to start that conversation. But, of course, how you do that may differ, depending on your home life and what sort of family or support system you have around you.

Firstly, think about one person in your life who you feel most comfortable doing this with. Is it your mum or best friend? Perhaps it is a teacher or a grandparent. Whoever it is, you have to be able to say that you trust them and feel positive about the idea of starting a conversation, even if it may be difficult.

Timing Is Everything!

It may sound silly, but if your parents are planning a huge holiday or gathering, you may want to think about avoiding speaking before these things happen. Your parents will be distracted in all the planning, and they may not be able to give you the attention and time you deserve. Of course, this would be no reflection on you, but remember, picking a better and more quiet time will be better for you all.

Prepare With Resources

What you will be talking with your trusted other about will likely be the catalyst for several questions. It won't be that they don't care, but there's every chance they won't **know** what terms you're referring to or what they mean to you personally. Don't take that as an insult, but terms and times change quickly, so you may want to come armed with resources to help them understand the information you're giving them.

Maybe this book could be useful in some way if you picked out bits you find the most helpful to you.

Remember Your Expectations

What do *you* want from this conversation? Is it just to get the initial, 'I am exploring my gender identity' statement out there? Or are you looking to request that your pronouns be changed? Maybe you want help shopping for clothes that are more suited to how you want to identify, or perhaps you might need some support speaking to your school or college about it all.

It doesn't have to be any or all of those things, but it's important to know what you want from your person or people, and it always helps set the right tone and keeps all of you on the same page too.

Don't go in with a huge list of requests, as it can overwhelm. What you've known or thought about for a while is going to be ***extremely*** new news to your trusted person/people, so start slowly and allow for you all to have that thinking space.

These conversations should be one of joy, not sadness.

Seek An Ally Of Support

It can be very helpful to confide in a friend who supports you, your identity, and your decision to explore it. That being said, would you feel better if they became your ally when it came to the difficult conversations? I'm not suggesting they be there for the talk, because that will be a moment you'll likely need for yourselves, but what about afterwards? The chances are that you'll need someone to turn to for support, so having a trusted ally could make all the difference.

Be Patient

As you have grappled with your identity for some time, your family or friends haven't. Allowing the time for them to process what is being said is important and be understanding when they make linguistic mistakes. It takes time to adjust to pronouns or different names, especially when your parents have known you to have different ones in the past.

Saying something such as, 'I understand it will take time; I just don't want you to do it on purpose,' will help you establish their errors while ensuring they remain positive about your decision.

Find Things In Common

Asking and expecting a parent who has known you as their little girl or little boy all your life to no longer consider you that way can be difficult for them. That doesn't mean they aren't accepting of your decision; it just means they need time.

Finding common ground can be a great way to soften the blow and form a solid relationship moving forward, and there are so many ways to do this. Asking them what aspects of their own personality aren't stereotypically male or female is a good way to get them thinking.

It could be a certain dress sense, interests or even their profession that don't define their gender that are good open topics of conversation that can help you find things in common, and in doing so, you can put across the idea that you aren't changing, you're just reaffirming who you always were.

How would you recover from a bad experience of opening up to someone trusted about your gender identity, only to be rejected in some way?

So you finally take the brave step and open up to someone about your gender identity, and it is met with confusion and negativity. Possibly tears, the silent treatment or the ever pleasant:

'This is just a phase.'

How do you feel? I'm pretty sure you feel lost, hurt, lonely and angry. Sometimes it can bring feelings of confusion and regret, and it may even make you question if you did the right thing or make you doubt yourself.

What do you do?

Firstly, time heals so many things. Hard to consider when you are in the thick of pain, but it is possible that time can calm the situation down and that your parents or carers may come to you with an apology, admitting their surprise at your news.

People who have known us all our lives know the 'us' who we have been for the past however many years. They've watched us laugh, cry, dance, be poorly, start school, walk for the first time, talk for the first time and generally be the boy or girl they were born as.

In some cases, the news that you want to talk about your gender identity, or indeed identify differently, can be like a bolt out of the blue. They may know less about gender identity than you now know, and they may need your help and understanding to try and understand **_you_** better. So this is an excellent opportunity to bond, find common ground and work through it together so they can support you.

In other cases, and unfortunately so, you may find yourself dealing with toxic behaviour, and because they are an authoritative figure, you may feel inclined to believe them or be swayed by their opinion or reaction. You may nod and agree and live their rules for an easy life.

There shouldn't be any rules when it comes to gender identity.

There is a totally different kind of hurt that comes from a parent who wants you to abide by their rules, beliefs and morals, and heaven forbid if we choose another way of life or a way of identifying that does not match their idea of correct, then it can be a horrid, horrid time.

Being young doesn't give you many options to leave home, as a young adult could do for work or university. You can find yourself living under the roof of rejection for many years before you get a chance to find your freedom, but that shouldn't damage your character and integrity.

This is where it is really important to build a life for yourself, slowly but surely. First, accept that you had a bad experience with a trusted person who should have been there and supported you but instead chose to reject your conversation and feelings.

If you can find another trusted person to open up to. Someone in your life who will be open and helpful to prove to you that there are always two sides to the coin.

Sometimes, sadly, we all have to face the reality that there are toxic people everywhere and that, even worse, there's a chance we could be related to one. This is something I had to realise about my own father for different reasons, but the reasons still hurt and still apply to me.

The one thing my father did for me was encourage me to be the sort of parent he never was. Yes, I could have been bitter and sad, and for a while, I wondered if there was something wrong with me until I stepped back and saw the bigger picture. When I did, I saw that he treated many people in his life the same way and caused much sadness, stress and anger within certain dynamics.

It was then I came to see the light fully. I needed to live my own life, my way, without the fear that he would criticise or mock me. I now do, and the journey here was hard. But, I sought therapy, saw many helpful YouTube videos, built my life from scratch, and have no regrets.

It can be the same for you after your bad experience. Then, you can be the person you are without the judgement of others.

Sometimes, recovering after these types of negative experiences can feel like climbing slowly uphill, in the rain, without a coat. The pain can outweigh the desire to feel better from it, but that's because we spend too much time focusing on the actual pain and not what comes next.

To compare, a friend of mine recently had a baby, and her husband left her ***three days*** after the birth. Several months later, she regularly calls me for a chat, and lately, she has been saying that she feels he left her because she's boring. I stopped her. 'Hang on,' I said. There is a huge difference between him being bored and you being boring.

Think about that.

There is a massive difference between your trusted other rejecting your conversation and you being a rejection.

A huge difference.

Number one, how can one person determine who you are and the person you now wish to identify as? Number two, how can their rejection of your news make you feel as though you are the rejection? Their actions towards your feelings are the only thing that should be discussed here.

When people we love and trust let us down, it can make us feel as though there is something wrong with us, as if *we* are the problem. In your case, you're going to feel as though your gender identity has come in the way of your relationship and that it is going to cause conflict if it hasn't already.

Truthfully speaking, not everybody is guaranteed to respond to your news in a way that empowers you and affects you positively, and at first, that might seem difficult and surprising. Soon enough, though, you'll find solace in good people, and you will create your own support system who will be there for you through the more challenging times.

As your identity becomes more established, and you adjust to life as this person you've always felt you were, instead of the one you were born with, other people will begin to see you in the same way. They'll see how happy you are, how comfortable you are in your own skin and how you are now living your best, most authentic life imaginable.

Strive for this, and strive for happiness. Love yourself hard, and make sure you never have a day off.

What about my school uniform or using public toilets?

Both are very valid questions when it comes to making decisions about how you want to be recognised in public. For example, you may feel highly uncomfortable wearing the uniform that has been assigned to 'girls' or 'boys.'

Luckily, many schools are recognising this and changing their rules to be more inclusive of all people, no matter how they identify. You should check your school policy for this; if you cannot see anything, speaking to a teacher may help you open doors not just for yourself but for other teenagers in your school who feel the same.

As for **toilets,** you may wish to use the toilets or changing rooms of your self-identified gender rather than of the sex assigned to you at birth. But, again, you should be supported by your school to do so, and speaking to a teacher or guidance counsellor within the school will help you in this matter.

This is actually a legal requirement under the Equality Act, and now more than ever, we are seeing gender-neutral toilets cropping up in public, as well as venues all across the country. So if you are in school and are thinking about this, find out your school policies, and speak to a member of staff.

Why Is Gender Identity Equality Important?

Well, it is so important that it has its own Act! The Equality Act 2010 legally protects people from discrimination in the workplace and in wider society. Before this, there were many laws that have basically been put together in one Act to make it easier to understand and, as a result, stronger.

Equality is about making sure each individual person has an equal opportunity to make the most of their lives. That shouldn't mean any different for those who choose to identify in ways other than they were born with. What a person believes, where they come from, the way they were born, or their race or religion should not be factored into consideration, and luckily now there are many ways in which these have been made illegal to do so.

When it comes to schools, each individual setting knows what works best for them and the different policies that carry the students well. The needs of the pupils and parents' wishes are listened to and taken into account, but there is no official dictation from the government on how this should work. Mostly that is down to the individual cases of each pupil.

Everything leads to one thing – acceptance. I think quite a bit about how much better the world would be if we all got along and accepted each other for who we are, but I know we still have a way to go.

Luckily, thanks to the Acts such as the Equality Act 2010, we are seeing more and more people defended during times of inequality and more powerful ways to recognise when mistakes are made. It is so important to protect the individual choices of other people so that we can all live the lives we were meant to without unnecessary judgement or consequence.

I'm Not Comfortable In The Body That I Have. What Can I Do?

Feeling as though you are stuck in a body that wasn't meant to be yours can feel like nature made a terrible mistake. Does that sound familiar to you at all? It can mean you might not like looking in the mirror at yourself or dressing in certain clothes because they show off parts of your body that you wish were not there.

The first thing you might want to consider is how you can make yourself feel better immediately. Do you like a particular type of clothing that you could wear more of, that will help you express yourself more? It can be something as simple as a colour or a t-shirt style. Baggy, fitted, going for a small or larger size are all good ideas to slowly start thinking about how you can feel more comfortable.

Another idea is looking at your hair. How can you express yourself with a small change? For example, you might want to experiment with a semi-permanent colour or a different style or cut. As you think about these things, you can experiment or look online to see what might suit you or what you like.

You might already be thinking about possible medication that could be offered to you. Still, a lot of that is defined by age and through individual needs, and you'll need to think carefully about when that timing is right, who can support you and also see your doctor.

Feeling this way about your body can bring on all sorts of emotions, such as anxiety or depression. If you can feel a bit of a shift in your mental health, you should reach out to speak to someone you trust.

These shifts in your mental health could see you retreat from social situations or not wanting to take part in activities such as sports at school for fear of feeling self-conscious.

Have you ever felt that way?

What if I were to say to you that so many people go through these feelings. You are at the age where your body is going through so many emotional and physical changes, and they can be difficult for teenagers who *don't* want to change their gender identity. It can be a shock to see parts of your body grow, develop hair, or for voices to change. To top it all off, spots can make a dramatic entrance, as well as sweat in all kinds of places. It's no wonder puberty is a stressful time, and you guys don't get enough support, in my honest opinion.

I know it is hard, and I can only imagine having a body that you don't feel should be yours.

As previously mentioned and suggested, there is strong advice in changing what you can control today. However, long term, you may want to explore other options that see your body physically change, and when that time comes, your doctor and trusted people in your life would be the first port of call.

Let me tell you that if you are embarrassed about speaking to your doctor, this will not be the first time that someone your age has gone to them with these wishes or concerns. It's their job to listen, advise and help.

They are on your side.

Helpful as the exercises were back when you worked through them, you could always revisit them during these more difficult times because they are there to support you and help you discover things about yourself that may previously have been hidden or tricky to untangle.

If you feel your mental health is slipping a little, or you don't feel like yourself, you should reach out. However, don't think that problems will go away if left untreated because sometimes we can bury issues when we needn't.

The same goes if you ever feel you want to harm yourself, as some people feel this is an effective way of coping. It isn't and can be very harmful to you.

Pause and reflect. What would it help you with? If you were tempted to do that sort of thing to yourself, is it going to make you like your body more? The answer is no. Temporarily, would it solve any issues, and long term, will it help a situation change for the better?

Again, very likely, no.

Reach out and speak to someone because I am 100% certain that you ***all*** have at least one person in your life who cares about you deeply, and they would be very hurt to know what pain you are in and that you are feeling so alone with it.

It is hard to make the first move and ask for help, and so many of us struggle to admit that we have these horrid thoughts about ourselves, our lives, or in your case, your gender identity. A common thought is that you are a burden or you're a problem if you speak up. Another thought could be that you feel someone might laugh at you or dismiss you in some way, and if that is the case, you've simply asked the wrong person for help.

Think carefully about your future, and remind yourself frequently that you will not be stuck in these thought patterns forever and that you will eventually find happiness within your body. If it isn't today, then find ways to express yourself that will help you today, such as my suggestions above, as they can help ease an element of pressure.

I am worried that any change in my gender identity will bring shame on my culture or community. How should I approach this?

Some cultures are more inclusive of gender identity and sexuality than others, but you must remember that different gender identities or sexualities are found in all cultures, races and religions. Some people within your own community may be against the changing of gender identity or same-sex attraction. Still, you mustn't forget that there will also be people who will be more inclusive and accepting of it.

With all that being said, it is unlikely you'll be reassured that everything is going to be alright if you have fears that your culture or community will find it difficult to accept or understand the sexual or gender identity you truly are. As a result, you may feel very isolated and unsure of where to turn for support.

It is helpful to look outside your community to find information and support. You can do this via your school counselling service or even your doctor. There are also many resources online that can guide you through your feelings and worries about potential backlash from your closer community or family.

The rules or beliefs behind religion can have the power to make you feel ashamed, as you feel as though you are going against them. You've done nothing wrong, and the common mistake of thinking that gender identity is something we simply choose or can control is a giant mistake. We don't choose to be who we are; we simply *are* who we are.

If your feelings of shame have become overwhelming, or you feel lost and fearful, reach out to someone outside your community for support. You aren't the first, and you certainly won't be the last.

Is It Normal To Feel Scared Of My New Identity?

I see this fairly frequently, and I am still surprised that so many people are surprised that they feel this way. There is a partial and logical explanation to the science behind being scared, which I will go through shortly, but before then, let's go to the actual question.

YES!

Of course, it is normal to be scared. As you delve deeper into your newly announced identity, you will be thinking about how you'll introduce yourself. You'll be thinking about how you express yourself and how your identity will match the idea of what you want it to physically represent. This is a time for exploration and experimentation, and sometimes you'll feel you're not getting it right.

There is no right or wrong where your gender identity is involved. If you wish to transition to a man or woman from the opposite sex, then yes, as comfortable as you will feel beginning to take on the clothing, or physicalities of doing so, you're likely still going to anticipate what the reaction will be from everyone else, and that can be scary.

Or what about identifying as non-binary? How will you dress or have your hair from day to day, and how will that be for people you know?

Much of the anticipation isn't about you, though, is it? If you think about it, what you could be scared about the most is being authentically you, with potential criticism coming from the outside.

If you ever change or have changed your pronouns, you might be anxious about people getting them wrong or having to correct those who do. How will you do it? Will they be mad or apologetic?

Losing yourself in the worry of what is to come is to take away the joy of the present moment.

The person you've evolved to become on this journey could be someone you've kept hidden for a long time through fear of shame and embarrassment, so if it takes you a while to get used to being that person, then that's okay.

Take it slowly, and enjoy the new experiences and friends you make and meet along the way.

Never be scared of being yourself.

How Can I Take Care Of Myself Through My Gender Identity Journey?

Prioritising your self-care is so important, but people who have been on or are going through a gender identity journey have a lot of reasons to practise looking after themselves. There is enough stress in this world, with friendships, school, college, homework, friends and family, but if you throw gender politics into the mix, that stress can quickly snowball, so you really need to take care of yourself.

As helpful as a nice bubble bath is, the sort of self-care I'm talking about goes a little deeper than that. I'm talking about the real things that build your emotional resilience for when those challenges really throw themselves at you.

Self-care, then, will look somewhat different for someone like you, whose gender expressions and/or identity can make you feel like you're an outsider sometimes. But, I want you to have joy in your life! So, specially compiled for you then are my three top ways to really look after yourself.

One - Style How You Want To Look

Starting with a nice affirming way to take care of yourself: be yourself. Even down to the colour or choice of clothing, it is all about how *you* want to look. You may have spent a lot of time growing up feeling that pressure to look a certain way that went against everything you felt and still feel about yourself. Developing your personal style and fully embracing it can be an incredible form of self-care!

If you are thinking about changing your look but you are a little apprehensive, reach out to any support system you have and have some fun going through different ideas together or having a look around the clothes shops. Maybe you could even do a clothes swap with them!

Two – Get Moving

Physical activity regulates our emotions, and it doesn't have to mean hitting a gym or anything remotely costly. When I am out for a walk, I forget what is going on in my life, or at the very least, I am able to sort out all my thoughts, as if I were organising a huge filing cabinet in my brain!

I don't really want your focus to be on a type of physical activity that is connected to diet culture because this isn't about weight or vanity; it's about doing something that makes you happy in a genuine way, whether that is swimming, running, biking, yoga, or even a simple lap around your neighbourhood.

If you are bringing a little happy dance (quite literally, if you wanted) into your day, then you're doing it right.

Three – Allow Yourself To Unplug

Below, I've given you some great places to visit online that are great places to start exploring the wider community of gender identity. There will be someone on the list who inspires and ignites a part of you, and if they don't, they're sure to lead you to places that will.

These pages and groups are open at all hours, so if you are struggling to sleep one random Wednesday, you can click and scroll to your heart's content. This 24-hour access, day in, day out, is not always good, especially when you can get caught up in strangers' ignorant opinions or comments on the internet.

Disconnect every once in a while, and unplug the cable.

You'll feel so much better.

When It All Gets A Bit Much

You won't always feel like doing something good for you, in particular on the days when you have a bad experience or when you witness or are subject to hearing something unkind. So, for example, getting up and forcing yourself to go for a walk every day may not be logistically viable for you to do, but if you can do one thing each day that somehow turns your mood around, then you should focus on that.

And you know what? If you want to make the most enormous cake with your friends and all watch your favourite film – then do that! Please just remember to send me a slice in the post.

Finally...

What Do I Want From My Life?

Remember that you are still young. If you put your gender identity to one side for a second, you can still appreciate that your mind can change frequently. What career you'd like, what you might like to study or do after school, and where you see yourself living. All these areas of life are to be explored, and it is fun to do so. These questions can seem open-ended at your age, but essentially, you're supposed to be young and finding out as you go along.

You might laugh, but it's actually normal to feel confused for no reason at all, and that's without your gender identity coming into play. You begin to realise a lot during this phase of your life, alongside coping with the biological changes occurring that you may or may not like at all, as these can interfere with the idea of you changing your own gender identity.

You aren't expected to make life-changing decisions at this point in your life, so there is no timeline to decide who you really are. If you experience bullying or discrimination at school because you might be a little different from what they deem as 'normal,' seeking support is the best thing you can do. In doing so, you give yourself permission to carry on being you, and the rest will fall into place.

You're going to want to be accepted. It's in all of our nature to be accepted by those around us. Whether they be friends, family, or people we meet in everyday life. We want to know that what we're saying and doing are the right things, and in turn, those good decisions are going some way to give us the life we want, but that isn't where it ends.

Acceptance

Let me tell you, the only person who needs to accept you is you. There are parts of us that are never going to be perfect. I know I still procrastinate more than I should, and it will always be an uphill battle, but I got through my life so far by just doing my best and believing and accepting myself fully.

What will help you the most, that I want to impress on all of you, is that part of your identity is saying no to things that you don't want to do. At your school, you're going to have many people telling you what you have to do or not do, but in life, it is your right to curate your life through your own perspective.

There is freedom in the choices you make about yourself, and the freedom to express who you are should not be met with fear or resistance because, eventually, that will catch up with you for all the wrong reasons. Letting go of what other people expect from you is going to really help you on your journey of figuring out what you want from life and turning your dreams into reality.

No matter what you want or who you are, taking care of your mental health should be your priority. Do not cave to peer pressure, and don't let any unkindness get the best of you.

If you can remember these things and go back to those exercises we talked about earlier, it'll be much easier to figure out what you want from life as it happens.

But there is no rush.

I hope you have found some of these questions relatable to you and that the answers have given you some clear thinking.

Below, as mentioned several times, are a list of places you can seek online for help, support or guidance.

Support Centre

You may use several of these areas for support, you may use one, or you may use none. Either way, along your journey, there may be times you feel overwhelmed and particularly alone, and that is what everything listed below is here for.

They are here for you.

So, reach out if you need to, and never feel that you're alone.

As you explore these pages and channels, you may stumble across more places of interest that suit you personally, and you should be encouraged to explore them responsibly. If something isn't good for you, then leave that channel and find an alternative. Life is too short to go down a rabbit hole that will end up leaving you feeling worried or sad, or worse yet, even more confused.

Time to be uplifted, and mostly *not* alone.

The Mix Gender Support – Support For Transgender Youth

The mix is there for you to listen to and help if you are confused about your own identity or sexuality. They can help you think more clearly. They are also there to help you understand the different issues trans young people face and where to go to get you the support you need. ***You can call them on 0808 8084994.***

www.themix.org/sexuality/trans

Youth Groups – Gendered Intelligence

This is a hub for teens to socialise, make friends, have fun and meet other trans, non-binary or gender questioning people in a safe place. They also run Online Youth Groups, which are there to help you feel less alone, talk to someone who is there specifically for you, and make online friends. ***Their support line is 0330 3559678.***

www.genderedintelligence.co.uk

The Be You Project

A charity that supports LGBTQ+ youth and has LOTS of help and advice for young people on their gender identity journey. They also support family and friends and are a good hub of resources for anyone making the gender identity journey or those who know someone who is.

www.thebeyouproject.co.uk

Samaritans

Open 24/7, Samaritans are always on the other end of a phone, no matter how big or small the issue is. They are there to listen and help you work through what's on your mind, with no judgement. ***Their number to call free is 116 123.***

www.samaritans.org

Facebook - Gender Dysphoria/Transgender Support

This private group helps and offers support in a safe and respectful place for people who are transgender OR have a transgender family member.

www.facebook.com/groups/693934297287443

Facebook - Support for LGBTQ+/Mental Health/Coming Out

This is another private group that offers help and support in a safe place for all people who need it. They have a zero tolerance for negative behaviour and endeavour to keep you safe. You can post your worries or fears about your journey, or coming out, or if you have problems surrounding your mental health.

www.facebook.com/groups/2120313621424954

Instagram – Tanya Compas - @tanyacompas

Tanya is an award-winning Youth Worker and has been recognised as one of the UK'S top 100 most inspiring women. Also, as head of youth engagement for @UKBlackpride (Instagram), Tanya's posts are equally as inspiring and send a great message to all.

www.instagram.com/tanyacompas

Instagram – Lottie L'Amour - @lottielamour

Lottie is a plus-size fashion, beauty and positivity blogger who uses her platform to discuss all things body positivity, self-expression and non-conformity. She is a real ray of sunshine!

www.instagram.com/lottielamour

YouTube - AMAZE org Channel

This YouTube Channel has incredible sections on both Mental Health and Gender Identity and Sexual Orientation. The videos are short and really helpful without getting too bogged down in the negatives. They help so many people your age to think a bit more about their feelings and know that they are not alone.

www.youtube.com/amazeorg

TikTok – Capri Campeau

Capri has many followers who find her videos honest and warm as she discusses various gender identities through the lens of her own bisexual binoculars. With over 250,000 followers and over 6 million video likes, she is one to follow for that cool, down-to-earth feel.

https://www.tiktok.com/@capricampeau

TikTok – Keara Graves

Similarly to Capri, Keara offers a look into her life living as a genderfluid person with they/she pronouns. She offers a humorous look into her life and thoughts, and many of you will relate.

https://www.tiktok.com/@keara.graves

Social Media Talk

Earlier in the book, I mentioned social media and how it can be used either well or not so well. I've ensured that the accounts I shared with you come from a responsible and friendly place. The groups are all private and run well; the personal accounts are positive and offer people like you the inspiration and strength to be yourself and celebrate it well.

You may stumble across negative comments online. They may make you feel angry, frustrated, or sad. They might embarrass you, and their sole aim is to make you feel all those things because they come from people who don't know enough about gender identity or have been taught that there is only one way to identify, and that is the person you were born as.

These are severely outdated thoughts and beliefs, but everyday society is fighting back. We are all different, and we have every right to identify however we want to however feels right. Nobody is allowed to sway your self-esteem, especially strangers online.

So, that being said, you need to stay safe online. I'm certainly not trying to sound like your parent, but I do want you to recognise when something doesn't make you feel good, so make sure you walk away when you see something uncomfortable and head towards the more positive posts that encourage you.

- A Note From Me -

Writing this book was the easy part. I wanted to be someone who offers their words, support and guidance to you in the hope that you can box it all up and take it with you on your journey.

The hard part was you picking up the book and deciding to read it. It took courage and strength to delve into what was previously an unknown world for you, especially as relatable as you find it.

There are so many ways to identify, and currently, we live in times where it is becoming more and more common for younger people like yourselves to decide the person they want to be without judgement. This world, though, will never be rid of it, and you may encounter this for yourself if you haven't already. I haven't asked you to do anything as forcefully as I am about to because this book was intended to be for you, in your own time, and if you feel comfortable. However, there is one thing you must do. Not for me, but for you.

In the face of adversity, you ***must*** remain true to yourself.

This isn't negotiable. Never, ever try to fit yourself into a box that isn't meant for you. In being authentically you, you are keeping in line with your morals and beliefs, and they also make you **you.** This is part of your identity as a whole and must never be forgotten.

That's the mistake many people make with gender identity, they assume it is the be-all and end-all, and that can lead to very worrying thoughts about how you, entirely, are made up of your gender identity.

There is much more to you. Funny, shy, witty, confident, kind, caring, passionate, creative, sporty, academic, talented musician, artist, keen lawyer to be, a teacher in the making, nurse, bricklayer. How you identify personifies you, but it does not have to define you.

Simply having the freedom to be you is your human right, and nobody can take that away from you.

The questions you worked on and read through the book may be relevant for you today, but the answers may change as you move in your journey. So this book is always here for you when you feel you need to dip back in.

This Book Has No Expiry Date

Remember, your journey is yours alone. It cannot be rushed or compared, it cannot be forced one way or another, and the opinions of others cannot change it. You are you, and you are the only person who knows what it feels like to be you. So make it your mission to accept yourself for who you truly are and find like-minded people who are also experiencing these wise and powerful thoughts.

Any time you feel alone or at a breaking point, find comfort in knowing that everything is temporary and that those feelings will pass. Find comfort in knowing you can be anything or anyone you want to be and that there is someone who can help you and support you to do that in this world. Sometimes they are family or friends; other times, they may be strangers on the other end of a phone or email, and sometimes they may be counsellors whose jobs are to listen and support you in a confidential setting.

What's next for you? Maybe you've thought about a difficult conversation you need to have with a family member or carer. Has this book given you the reassurance you need that it will be okay?

None of our lives are problem free, and yours is and will be no different. You will experience injustices and unfair treatment. People tease and mock, and others will ignore you for no reason. This happens regardless of age, gender identity, race or religion. The world can be incredibly shallow, as society plays catch up with the changes it is seeing on a daily basis, and that has nothing to do with you or how you feel you need to identify. These are universal issues that people fight for the rights for, and you may find yourself doing so one day.

You also have much to celebrate. You're an amazing person, and your future is yours for the taking. You're part of the next generation, and you matter.

Thank you so much for reaching out and doing something for you. It has meant a great deal to me to be in a position to write it, knowing that the words, exercises, and guidance could help some of you in some way.

You completing something like this book is a huge win for you because it means you've taken the

time to process your feelings and emotions and what it is you want from here on out. I hope it has left you feeling as empowered and awesome as you actually are. Settle for nothing less.

Be proud. Live your life well. Be safe.

Be you.

Printed in Great Britain
by Amazon